AWAKEN HEALING ENERGY THROUGH THE TAO

THE TAOIST SECRET OF CIRCULATING INTERNAL POWER

by Mantak Chia

AURORA PRESS

First published in 1983 by
Aurora Press
P.O. Box 573
Santa Fe, New Mexico 87504

ISBN: 0-943358-07-8
Library of Congress Catalogue Card No:
83-71473

Mantak Chia

ACKNOWLEDGEMENTS

I wish to express my gratitude to my many students, who so willingly devoted their time and effort in practice. I wish also to thank them for consenting to be interviewed so that others might know what they experienced and how they were helped through this practice.

I want to thank Dr. Lawrence Young, attending physician at New York Infirmary-Beekman Downtown Hospital and a private internist, Dr. C. Y. Hsu, physician-in-charge of the Acupuncture and Nerve Block Clinic at Albert Einstein College of Medicine, Stephen Pan, Ph.D., Director of East Asian Research Institute, and H. Reid Shaw attorney, who are actively engaged in presenting my work to the medical community.

I wish to offer my appreciation to Sam Langberg, for his understanding and untiring work in editing the first edition. Sam Langberg is a freelance writer and a Taoist Esoteric Yoga instructor living in the New York area. He has been practicing Yoga for over 10 years, and currently works with the Taoist Esoteric Yoga Center writing classbooks and other materials.

Many thanks go to Michael Winn and Robin Winn for long months spent revising and expanding the second edition. I thank Susan MacKay who revised our Taoist Esoteric Yoga sitting figure. Special thanks go to my secretary JoAnn Cutrera for her patience in typing and retyping the manuscript.

Finally, I am grateful to my wife, Maneewan Chia, whose suggestions and encouragement in this, as in all matters, have always been valuable to me.

TABLE OF CONTENTS

List of illustrations *i*

Foreward by Gunther Weil, Ph.D. *iii*

INTRODUCTION: What Is The Healing Energy of the Tao?

 By Michael Winn *vii*

About the Author *xi*

A Commentary on Western Medicine and Taoist Yoga

 By Lawrence Young M.D. *xiii*

PART I:
Practical Steps to Awaken Your Own Healing Energy

Chapter 1: AWAKEN THE "CHI" LIFE ENERGY 1

  The Primary Energy Channels 4

  Proper Wiring of the Etheric Body 4

  What Does It Mean to "Open the Routes"? 5

  Lessen Side Effects by Careful Preparation 5

  Acupuncture and the Microcosmic Orbit 6

  Summary. 7

Chapter 2: PREPARE TO CIRCULATE THE CHI ENERGY 9

  Create a Relaxed Environment 9

  How to Sit 11

  How to Breathe 13

  Mental Attitude 14

  Position of the Tongue 15

Chapter 3: THE SECRET OF THE INNER SMILE 17

  The Healing Power of a Smile 17

  Smile Love Into Your Vital Organs 19

  How to Smile Down with the Inner Smile 21

  Front Line. 22

  Middle Line: Swallow Saliva into Lower Abdomen. 26

  Back Line: Spine 26

  End by Collecting the Energy 27

  Practice the Inner Smile in Daily Life 27

PART II:
CIRCULATE HEALING ENERGY IN THE MICROCOSMIC ORBIT

Chapter 4: BEGIN THE ORBIT: OPEN THE FRONT CHANNEL,

  THE FUNCTIONAL 31

  Awaken the Individual Healing Points 33

  Choosing Your First Point: The Navel 33

  Use a Finger to Help Concentrate 34

  Heart and Chest Problems 35

  High Blood Pressure 35

  Low Blood Pressure. 36

  Gastro-Intestinal Problems. 37

  The Second Energy Center: Kuan-Yuan

    or Jing /Gong/Ovarian or Sperm Palace 38

  The Third Energy Center: Hui-Yin/Perineum 40

Chapter 5: OPEN THE BACK CHANNEL: THE GOVERNOR ..43
The Fourth Energy Center: Chang-Chiang/Coccyx 44
The Fifth Energy Center: Ming-Men 45
Back Pain 45
The Sixth Energy Center: Chi-Chung 46
Stimulate the Pancreas 47
Upper Back Pain 48
The Seventh Energy Center: Yu-Chen 48
The Eighth Energy Center: Pai Hui 48
The Ninth Energy Center: Yin-Tang 49

Chapter 6: COMPLETE THE MICROCOSMIC ORBIT 53
Beginners: Reverse the Chi Flow 55
The Tenth Energy Center: "Heavenly Pool"/
    Tongue to Palate 56
The Eleventh Energy Center: Hsuan-Chi/Throat 57
The Twelfth Energy Center: Shun-Chung/Heart 58
The Thirteenth Energy Center:
    Chun-Kung/Solar Plexus 58
Collect the Energy When Finished 59
Rubbing the Face 60

Chapter 7: OPEN THE ARM AND LEG ROUTES: THE LARGE
    HEAVENLY CYCLE 61

PART III: PRACTICAL POINTERS

Chapter 8: SET A TRAINING SCHEDULE 69
Review: The Major Points of the Microcosmic Orbit ...70
Circulate Chi Power Continuously in the Orbit 73
The Final Goal is Automatic Circulation of Chi 74

Chapter 9: THE SAFETY VALVES: HOW TO PREVENT
    SIDE EFFECTS 77
The Cleansing Process: Belching and Diarrhea 78
Sexual Life During Practice 78
Appetite and Stomach Ailments...................79
Throat Center: Coughing 79
Cleansing of the Esophagus, Stomach
    and Intestines 79
Illusions and Mental Illness 80
When To See a Doctor...........................81
Proper Practice Will Prevent Side Effects............81

Chapter 10: COMMONLY ASKED QUESTIONS AND ANSWERS
    ON THE MICROCOSMIC 83
  1. What is chi? 83
  2. Do you have to sit on a chair? 84
  3. What to do when erection or vaginal expansion
     occurs during practice?.....................85
  4. Will circulating the microcosmic
     help my sexual problems?...................86
  5. Is Taoist practice suitable for everyone?..........86
  6. Can women practice during menstruation? 87

7. Should I concentrate on the "third eye"
   between the eyebrows? 87
8. Why do some practitioners develop back or
   shoulder pain? 87
9. Can people that have had surgery practice? 88
10. Why do some people experience
    ringing in the ears? 89
11. What to do for loss of appetite after practice? 89
12. Why do some people shift about, shake their legs,
    or make sounds during practice? 90
13. How does chi affect the sick body? 92
14. How to remedy energy blockage in the chest? 93
15. What is the proper time to practice? 93
16. Do you need to change your diet? 94
17. Does practicing the microcosmic affect
    your interests in social life? 94
18. Can practice cut down on the number of hours
    you sleep? 95
19. Should you practice when angry,
    sad, or disappointed? 95
20. Does rhythmic breathing and chanting
    help to circulate the microcosmic? 96
21. Does Master Chia pass energy to help
    open the routes? 97
22. Are there any side effects with
    the Taoist method? 97
23. Why do I feel tired after meditation? 98
24. What is the benefit of completing
    the microcosmic? 99

PART IV:
HEALING APPLICATIONS OF THE TAO ENERGY
Chapter 11: MEDICAL SCIENCE LOOKS
            AT THE MICROCOSMIC 103
   A Medical Opinion on the Benefit of
   Taoist Chi Circulation
      by C. Y. Hsu, M.D. 103
   A Brief History of Taoism and the Healing Arts
      by Stephen Pan, Ph.D. 104
   A Doctor's Search for the Taoist Healing Energy
      by Lawrence Young, M.D. 107
Chapter 12: PERSONAL EXPERIENCES WITH
            THE MICROCOSMIC 111
   Tape Recorded in Workshops with Mantak Chia and
   Gunther Weil
Chapter 13: AN M.D. INTERVIEWS THREE PRACTITIONERS
            OF TAOIST YOGA 123
      by Lawrence Young, M.D. 123
   An Interview with S. 123

An Interview with Dan 127
An Interview with Bill 131

PART V:
BEYOND THE MICROCOSMIC

Chapter 14: OBSERVATIONS ON HIGHER
          TAOIST PRACTICES 139
Taoist Yoga and the Kundalini By Michael Winn 141

Chapter 15: SUMMARY OF THE SEVEN STAGES
          OF TAOIST ESOTERIC YOGA 149
The Small Heavenly Cycle (Microcosmic) 149
The Seven Formulas of the Seven Books of the Tao . . .151
1. First Formula: Fusion of the Five Elements 151
2. Second Formula: Lesser Enlightenment
        of Kan and Li 154
3. Third Formula: Greater Enlightenment
        of Kan and Li 155
4. Fourth Formula: Greatest Enlightenment
        of Kan and Li 156
4. Fifth Formula: Sealing of the Five Sense Organs 157
6. Sixth Formula: Congress of Heaven
        and Earth Immortality 158
7. Seventh Formula: Reunion of Heaven and Man.
        True Immortal Man. 158
Chart of the Complete Taoist
        Esoteric Yoga System .160

Chapter 16: COMPLEMENTARY TAOIST PRACTICES 163
Taoist Esoteric Yoga Course Offerings 163
Seminal and Ovarian Kung-Fu 168
Iron Shirt Chi Kung 169

APPENDIX

    A. TABLE OF ENERGY CENTERS 174
        Chakras, Acupuncture Points, Taoist Energy Centers
    B. HOW TAOIST YOGA AFFECTS YOUR
        HORMONAL SYSTEM 183

LIST OF ILLUSTRATIONS

Diagram 1 The Human Fetus — 3
Diagram 2 Rub the Feet — 10
Diagram 3 Sitting Position — 11
Diagram 4 Hand Position — 12
Diagram 4a Sitting Position — 13
Diagram 5 Breathing — 13
Diagram 6 Tongue Positions — 15
    a. Wind Position
    b. Fire Position
    c. Water Position
Diagram 7 The Inner Smile — 18
Diagram 8 Front Line Smile — 23
Diagram 9 Middle Line Smile — 24
Diagram 10 Back Line Smile — 24
Diagram 11 Points & Energy Centers — 32
Diagram 12 High Blood Pressure — 36
Diagram 13 Low Blood Pressure — 37
Diagram 14 The First Energy Center — 38
Diagram 15 The Second Energy Center — 39
Diagram 16 The Third Energy Center — 41
Diagram 17 The Back Channel — 44
Diagram 18 The Fourth Energy Center — 45
Diagram 19 The Fifth Energy Center — 46
Diagram 20 The Small Heavenly Cycle — 54
Diagram 21 The Tongue Links the Flow — 55
Diagram 22 Energy Flows Through Palate — 56
Diagram 23 11th, 12th & 13th Energy Centers — 57
Diagram 24 Collect Energy at the Navel — 59
    a. For Men
    b. For women
Diagram 25 Fubbing the Face — 60
Diagram 26 The Leg Route — 63
Diagram 27 The Large Heavenly Cycle — 64
Diagram 28 The Large Heavenly Cycle — 65
Diagram 29 The Microcosmic Orbit — 75
Diagram 30 Bursts of Chi — 90
Diagram 31 Complementary Taoist Practices — 171
Diagram 32 Points & Energy Centers — 182
Diagram 33 The Endocrine Glands — 186
Diagram 34 The Pituitary Gland — 193

FOREWORD
By Gunther Weil, Ph.D.

During the last twenty-five years the United States and Western Europe has witnessed an amazing growth of popular interest in a multitude of personal growth and wholistically based health disciplines. The West once again has become a "melting pot" but this time the cauldron contains a mixture of the sacred traditions of the East as well as some of the emerging internal technologies of the body, mind and spirit. This movement, known generally as the "New Age", is characterized by popular magazines and a sizable growing literature, a large number of spiritually oriented groups and a rapidly growing consumer market for wholistically based medicine and other "appropriate technologies". We are clearly seeing a major shift in attitudes and values in our relationships to our inner lives and our responsibilities for the future of the planet Earth.

Parallel with these developments we can also see emerging a scientific picture of the universe that resembles the classic world view of the major oriental religions. The scientific picture that is developing at the end of the 20th century is less linear, less deterministic and less reductionistic in the frontier sciences of physics and biology. This picture becomes increasingly similar to the intuitive, phenomenological and process/interactive model of man-in-the-universe that has characterized Chinese philosophy and science for thousands of years.

These two trends, the growth of "New Age" consciousness and the shift in our scientific paradigms are beginning to converge in some practical ways in the field of wholistically inspired medicine. Perhaps the best example of this is the therapeutic modality of Acupuncture, one of the most powerful techniques in the classical Chinese medical system. A little known fact about Acupuncture and Chinese medicine is the enormous debt these systems owe to Taoist Esoteric Yoga. In fact, Taoist Esoteric Yoga is the mother of Chinese medicine as well as many other systems of healing and self-development.

For many Westerners Taoism has seemed an elusive and inscrutable path, best exemplified by the oracular mysteries of the I-Ching and the wisdom of Lao Tzu and Chuang Tsu, the nature philosophers of "The Way". For those interested in the Oriental healing or martial arts there are disciplines as Macrobiotics or Tai

Chi Chuan, but the nature of this relationship is far from clear. To suggest a connection between these and other practices and an esoteric core of Taoism is to confuse matters even further. In fact, the concept of an esoteric or inner core of Taoism is itself a new idea for New Age audiences. What sense are we to make of an esoteric foundation for a tradition that already seems so difficult to comprehend, especially in its practical ramifications?

By contrast, we are reasonably comfortable with the major concepts and methods of the various Indian meditation and yoga systems which began to find a place in our society in the 1920's. We have also come to appreciate the powerful systems of Buddhist thought and practice, especially Zen and Tibetan Buddhism which began to emerge into popular consciousness in the 1960's. But what about Taoism? What do we really know about this tradition other than a few fragments of the wisdom of the I-Ching, the Tao Teh Ching and a few other pieces of disconnected fragments of practical knowledge contained in the systems of Chinese medicine and martial arts? How can we begin to understand the contemporary practical applications of this ancient system of healing and spiritual development? What form must this knowledge take in order to enter the mainstream of our technological society at this time in our evolutionary transition?

The book by Master Mantak Chia addresses these questions and represents, to the best of my knowledge, the first opportunity for a Western audience to really grasp and digest the essential and practical aspects of Taoist Esoteric Yoga. Master Chia has performed an invaluable service through his efforts to present these ancient psychophysical methods in a form and sequence that corresponds to our contemporary scientific and technological world view. The information in the book, the first in a forthcoming series on Taoist Esoteric Yoga principles and methods, clearly describes the theory and practice of the Microcosmic Orbit, the foundation teaching of the entire Taoist system. Through their meditation experience and accumulated wisdom the ancient Taoist masters learned the importance of the free circulation of Chi energy in the body, both as a therapeutic technique for self-healing as well as a safety valve for preventing the side effects that often accompany the powerful experiences of Kundalini energy release. Master Chia, a true heir to the ancient Taoist system, has taken this information and broken it down into a systematic form of instruction that anyone can easily grasp and apply.

I believe that this book is an historically important contribution to the introduction of practical Taoism to the West. "Awaken Healing Energy Through The Tao" will help to evolve our understanding of the mind/body relationship in our healing practices as well as our scientific models of the energy structure of the human body.

INTRODUCTION:
WHAT IS THE HEALING ENERGY
OF THE TAO?
By Michael Winn

In the sixth century B.C., Lao-Tse began his classic essay, the Tao Te Ching, with this admonition: "The Tao which can be spoken of is not the Tao." Loosely translated, "Tao" means "the way" or "the power". In early Chinese writings the Tao implied an understanding of life which stressed individual harmony with the forces of nature. The Taoist sages often became hermits that lived in the mountains and disdained offers of power from admiring emperors, saying they preferred the "Ruler of Nature" to the transitory "Ruler of Society."

In the same tradition, "Awaken Healing Energy Through The Tao" is rooted in the process of nature, our bodily nature. This healing energy works independent of any particular belief or current scientific concepts. It differs from the Taoist religions which grew up around the original philosophy. In a nutshell, it is a subtle but verifiable experience of life energy, of "chi" flowing through the body in a specific pattern. It was discovered by practical-minded Chinese sages, and is available to to any person of any age who cares to train themselves to observe and use it. That this healing power is compatible with different individual beliefs or religions is apparent in the fact that the author Mantak Chia, is himself a Christian, but has used the traditional Taoist methods to help thousands of people heal or improve themselves.

A person could study hundreds of volumes of the Taoist Encyclopedia in Chinese and commentaries on the Tao Te Ching or I-Ching in a dozen languages without ever learning how to awaken the much poeticized healing power of the Tao. It would be far more useful for such a seeker to spend their time practicing the circulation of the healing life force in the "small heavenly cycle" or "microcosmic orbit" as described in this book.

Mantak Chia has read those hundreds of esoteric volumes, in addition to receiving the highest oral teaching from Taoist Masters. He believes the oral teachings are too important to be practiced by a lucky few only, hidden from other seekers by vague poetry or the arcane symbols of ancient writings. Master Chia sees that the age has come when the public needs and deserves a clear teaching of this healing power, which was shrouded in China by the same secrecy that surrounded medieval alchemy in Europe. This historical similarity is no accident, as the Taoist "Microcosmic Orbit" is a process of human alchemy, the first step towards transformation of human energy into its purest form. This distillation of a healing energy was perfected by generations of sages who spent their entire lives refining its many applications.

These applications to daily life are indeed enormous. It is not an exaggeration to say the circulation of human energy or "chi" throughout the body is also the key principal functioning behind much Chinese genius. It is responsible for Chinese achievements in medicine (acupuncture), the martial and meditative arts (Kung Fu, Tai Chi Chuan, Pa Kua Palm, Hsing I Chuan, Inner Alchemy), inspiration for a vast treasure of poetry and philosophy (I Ching, Tao Te Ching). It could be argued that the increased health and creative intelligence of the Taoist practitioners helped stimulate the impressive early Chinese advances in technology and government. Confucius was well versed in Taoist philosophy and expressed great admiration for it; he may well have been a practitioner of the art as well.

Since publication of the first edition of "Awaken Healing Energy Through The Tao", students of various Chinese arts have come to Mantak Chia and confessed they were shocked to see his book sold in a store. Its information was taught to them only after years of dedication and discipline in their practice, be it Tai Chi, meditation, or martial arts. They were told circulation of the microcosmic orbit was the "highest secret" to gaining internal power in the mind and body, and not to be revealed to those outside the "inner circle".

Having mastered many different systems of esoteric Chinese knowledge, Master Chia's perspective is different from most other teachers. For Master Chia, education begins with the awakening of this healing energy. It is the most important building block. If you master the circulation of your energy, growth in other disciplines proceeds more quickly. Opening the main channel of energy circulation in the body (referred to as the "microcosmic orbit" in this book) is analagous to a first grader learning to write the letters of the alphabet.

Without first learning how to write the alphabet, one cannot create words, sentences, paragraphs, or the simple and complex ideas taught up to the university level. It is the same with the healing power of the Tao. Without "getting" the flow of energy taught in this book, the practitioner will find it difficult to advance quickly to higher levels in related disciplines. Or, you may spend years with less direct methods in order to achieve the same end, e.g. repeat certain physical movements until the flow one day "arrives", sit facing a wall for 20 years, or repeat a mantra for a lifetime.

Later volumes of Master Mantak Chia's "Taoist Esoteric Yoga Encyclopedia" will elucidate some of the more advanced forms of Taoist practice in healing, meditation, and self-defense, and their application in balancing the forces which daily buffet us about. Seminal Kung Fu (a sexual practice for man) and Ovarian Kung Fu (a sexual practice for woman) reveals the Taoist secrets of transforming raw sexual energy into creative energy. Iron Shirt Chi Kung strengthens the whole body fascia, organs, tendons and bones and shows how to "root" the human energy in the earth. Fusion of the Five Elements" teaches how to transmute emotions, heal damaged organs and gain greater balance and insight into oneself. Tai Chi Chi Kung, Pa Kua Chi Kung and Palm, Hsing I Chi Kung, Death Touch Dan Mu, and Five Finger Kung Fu, build internal power, improve body alignment, and enable one to more quickly master the longer forms of Tai Chi Chuan, Pa Kua Palm, and Hsing I Chuan.

"Awaken Healing Energy Through The Tao" is scientific in that it demystifies some of the principles on which the miracle of self-healing and other feats of energy are based. At the same time it is deeply rooted in an ancient tradition of spiritual self-mastery that, step by step, leads the practitioner to experiencing the full mystery of the Tao.

March 31, 1983
New York City

Michael Winn is general editor of the Taoist Esoteric Yoga Encyclopedia.

ABOUT THE AUTHOR — Mantak Chia

The author of this book, Mantak Chia, was born in Thailand on April 4, 1944. When he was six or seven years of age he learned to "sit and still the mind" from Buddhist monks while on a summer vacation. This is not to say that he was passive and quiet as a child. In fact, he excelled in track and field events during his grammar school days in Hong Kong. It was during that time that he learned the traditional Thai Boxing and met Master Lu, who taught him Tai Chi Chuan. Shortly thereafter, Master Lu introduced him to Aikido, Yoga and more Tai Chi. His knowledge of esoteric practice did not begin, however, until he was eighteen and he had returned to Thailand. It was at that time that a senior classmate, Cheng Sue Sue, a student of Yi-Eng, taught him the level of Tao Esoteric practice up to the Reunion of Man and Heaven.

When he was in his twenties, Master Chia studied with Master Meugi in Singapore, who taught him Kundalini Yoga and the Buddhist Palm. With the Buddhist Palm, he was soon able to eliminate blockages of flow of life-force in his internal organs and to drive cold, wet or sick energy out of patients who came to see his Master, thereby restoring them to health. The young Mantak Chia felt, however, that Kundalini Yoga produced too much heat and could be dangerous and so he later combined it with elements of Taoist practice, which had cooling effects.

Later, in his twenties, he met and studied with Master Pan Yu, who had created a synthesis out of Taoist, Buddhist and Ch'an teaching, and Master Cheng Yao-Lung, who had also created a new system by combining Thai Boxing and Kung Fu. From Master Cheng Yao-Lung, he learned the Shao-Lin secret method of internal power as well as the Iron Shirt method called "Cleansing the Marrow and Renewal of the Tendon". From Master Pan Yu, he learned a variation of Kundalini and the "steel body", a technique that is said to keep the body from decay. Master Pan Yu still lives and practices in Hong Kong, where he treats patients by transmitting his life-force to them. To better understand the mechanism behind the healing energy, Chia also studied Western medical science and anatomy for two years.

Yet, with all of these achievements, Master Chia was the manager of the Gestetner Company in Thailand, was in charge of sales of offset machines and was well acquainted with the working of the company's copying and printing machines. He may well be the only Taoist master in the world with a computer in his living room. He is also married and has a son. His wife Maneewan works as a medical technician. He is, in short, living proof that his practice is very much down-to-earth, striving to enhance everyday life and not requiring retreat from society to a hermit's life.

The main thrust of Chia's intention is to strip away the mysticism, the mumbo-jumbo, the powers vested in the Guru, the reliance on things-other-worldly or magical. He seeks to present, instead, a fully predictable working model that might be considered as a scientific means of dealing with energy systems. In time, he hopes this will lead to technological developments that might serve to simplify or speed the means whereby such progress might be made. It is with such hopes that he beckons members of the medical community to investigate what he has to offer. There are already physicians and lawyers and computer programmers, who have experienced, first hand, the benefits that Master Chia's methods provide. It is up to them and others in the scientific community to join Master Chia in his lifetime task of bridging the gap between reason and spirit, mind and body, science and religion.

A COMMENTARY ON WESTERN MEDICINE AND TAOIST YOGA

By Lawrence Young, M.D.

Since the publication of the first edition of Mantak Chia's book, "Awaken Healing Energy Through The Tao", hundreds of Americans from all walks of life in cities across the U.S. have reportedly experienced sensations of energy flow in the Microcosmic Circulation and in other parts of the body. The descriptions of these energy flow sensations match those described in many classical Chinese writings, most of them Taoist. I have also examined recent scientific electrophysiological studies on the acupuncture meridians, and both the Chinese and French scientists have in separate experiments proven that the acupuncture meridians do actually exist as a electrophysiological phenomenon and the scientific mapping of the acupuncture points and meridians has a 80-90% correspondence to the acupuncture map passed down in Chinese history for thousands of years.

In addition, stimulations of the appropriate acupuncture points actually produced neuro-endocrine secretions, measurable physiological changes in the intestinal, cardiac and other internal organ activities, electroencephalographic changes, and measurable electrical impulses received at the cerebral cortex of the brain. Deep connections of the acupuncture meridians to the internal organs have also been proven by separate experiments in China and in France.

It now becomes clear to me that the energy flow sensations experienced in Taoist Esoteric Yoga are the same as the "Qi sensation" experienced by patients during needle acupuncture, laser acupuncture or even accupressure. The Microcosmic Circulation is the Tu Mai and Ren Mai, the two most important and useful "curious meridians" in acupuncture. Taking the experience of his students as a whole, practically all of the acupuncture meridians have been felt by Mantak Chia's students. The same conclusion had been alluded to in several classical acupuncture texts. However, due to the lack of scientific evidence proving the validity of acupuncture, and the lack of scientific evidence proving the physiological changes in relaxation meditation and yoga, both acupuncture and Taoist Esoteric Yoga were considered as Chinese folklore and superstitions until now.

The work of Herbert Benson, M.D., Prof. at Harvard University Medical School, and several other scientists have gone a long way to change the above-mentioned misconceptions. Through careful experiments, they have proven that the Relaxation Response produces significant and beneficial physiological changes in the human body. Relaxation therapy and stress management has now become a respectable therapeutic modality in the medical circle.

Taoist Esoteric Yoga is of course by itself unique, a one-of-a-kind attempt at attaining supreme knowledge. However, we scientists like to dissect everything that we can lay our hands on. If we dissect the technology of Taoist Esoteric Yoga, we can say that the physiological effects of Taoist Esoteric Yoga is a product derived from the interaction of the physiological effects of Relaxation Response and the physiological effects of acupuncture. Relaxation Response quiets the electrical activities of the cerebral cortex and the rest of the central nervous system to such a point that the acupuncture energy (Qi, chi, prana) can start to flow smoothly and freely again.

My observation is that excessive electrical activities of the cerebral cortex retards the generation and the flow of acupuncture energy (Qi, chi, prana). Furthermore, quieting the electrical activities in the cerebral cortex allows the sensations of Qi to flow to come into conscious awareness of the Taoist Yoga practitioner, so that the practitioner can now begin to consciously generate more Qi and consciously guide its flow to remove obstructions and balance excesses and deficiencies in the acupuncture meridians and internal organs of his own body. This particular view of Taoist Esoteric Yoga also fits into the framework of Biofeedback, which means bringing your own physiological processes into your conscious mind and consciously manipulating them. According to my dissection, Taoist Esoteric Yoga is Relaxation Response Acupuncture and Biofeedback, three in one.

Now, what is the physical nature of Qi (prana, acupuncture energy)? What is the material structure of the acupuncture points and meridians? Numerous scientists all over the world are working on an answer to the above questions, but I do not think that there will be an answer for at least 10 to 20 years.

Do we have to wait another 10 to 20 years before using Taoist Esoteric Yoga to benefit mankind? No, for in the last few thousand years, numerous Chinese have already healed their own illnesses with Taoist Esoteric Yoga. And in the last 10 years a large number of hospitals and medical schools in China have officially adopted Qi Gong as one modality in the treatment of cancer, arthritis, hypertension and many other medical conditions, and they have claimed good results in their medical journals and publications. Classical Chi Kung (or Qi Gong, the official Chinese translation) is one aspect of Taoist Esoteric Yoga. However, the Qi Gong used in the Chinese hospitals and medical schools these days have overemphasized the physical exercise and breathing exercise components of Taoist Esoteric Yoga (equivalent to Hatha Yoga and Pranayama) and have ignored the need for Relaxation Response and Biofeedback and the need to consciously generate and guide Qi flow.

Taoist Rejuvenation Exercises and Taoist Breathing Exercises (equivalent to Hatha Yoga and Pranayama) as adopted by the Chinese hospitals and medical schools and called ''Qi Gong'' is no doubt an important step to promote acupuncture energy flow and to balance excesses and deficiencies of acupuncture energy. But all the classical Taoist texts and all of the living masters of the Taoist Esoteric Yoga tradition also emphasize the need for the Relaxation Response and Biofeedback components and the need to consciously generate and guide Qi flow. I understand that Mantak Chia and Herbert Benson, M.D. are going to China soon to lecture on the Relaxation Response and to exchange with the Chinese hospitals and medical schools information on Qi Gong. I hope that their visit will bring back an emphasis on Relaxation Response and Biofeedback in the Chinese Qi Gong programs.

That Relaxation Response, Biofeedback, Hatha Yoga and Yogic breathing exercises are important foundations of Taoist Esoteric Yoga is clear from my observations on Mantak Chia's students in the last year. Since the publication of the first edition of this book, many students of Yoga, Tai Chi, T-M and other meditation traditions have come to study with Mantak Chia. Those with 4 to 5 years prior experience with the Relaxation Response. Hatha Yoga and related disciplines felt the acupuncture energy flow instantly, or in a matter of days, opened up many channels and felt the Qi energy more vividly and intensely. Those without such prior experience took many more weeks and months before they could feel the Qi flow. They felt the acupuncture energy much less vividly, less intensely and less precisely in the acupuncture meridians.

In short, since the publication of the first edition of this book, I can see that the United States is fertile soil for the development of Taoist Esoteric Yoga into a respectable and important therapeutic modality. This is because Relaxation Response, Hatha Yoga and Acupuncture have already become household words in the United States in the last decade and they are the very basis of Taoist Esoteric Yoga.

Furthermore, Mantak Chia, a living heir to this valuable tradition, is selflessly and generously giving away all the heretofore preciously-guarded secrets to anyone willing to learn. I predict that Taoist Esoteric Yoga will soon be accepted by the medical community as one of the modalities in the treatment of cancer, arthritis, and any other illness that has something to do with the immune, the neuroendocrine and the regenerative functions of the human body.

Lawrence Young, M.D.
March 31, 1983

Lawrence Young, M.D. is an internist in private hospital and office practice in New York City. He was Chief Editor of *Report of the National Clearinghouse for Meditation*; Relaxation and Related Therapies. He authored a scientific paper entitled, "The Microcosmic Circulation — A Little Known Phenomenon And Its Therapeutic Implications", which he presented at the American Holistic Medical Association annual meeting in June 1981. He presented to the International Conference on World Medicine (organized by the Institute for Advanced Research in Asian Science and Medicine) in March 1982 a scientific paper entitled: "Prana Acupuncture — A New Frontier For Basic Science And Clinical Research".

PART I:

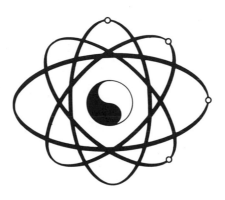

Practical Steps To Awaken
Your Own Healing Energy

CHAPTER 1

AWAKEN THE "CHI" LIFE ENERGY

Meditation, properly speaking, is the stilling of the mind. Most of the meditation techniques taught today still the mind using one of two basic approaches. The first is the Zen approach of "silent sitting", facing a blank wall until the mind becomes blank. You sit until the moment of pure awareness arrives, even if it takes twenty years. The second is the Mantra approach, in which the mind is rhythmically lulled to sleep with sounds or images. After thousands of repetitions the body begins to vibrate at a higher frequency, and the meditator becomes aware of the higher energies operating beyond the sensory process functions of our daily mind.

The Esoteric Taoist approach is different. It does not depend on total absence of the flux of thought. Instead, this system stresses the circulation of energy called "chi" along certain pathways inside the body. These pathways help direct the "chi" — also known as prana, sperm or ovarian power, the warm current, or kundalini power — to successively higher power centers (chakras) of the body. The secret of circulating this "chi" has been transmitted for thousands of years in China, where it brought extraordinary improvements in health and life.

But what is this "chi", and where does it come from? The chi is the primordial life force itself. It begins in human life with the piercing of an egg by a sperm cell. From this original fusion an enormously complex new human being develops. "Chi" is the continuous flow of energy linking the various tissues, organs and brain functions into a unified whole — a person. Chi also links this person to his environment.

The main channels of "chi" energy flow in the body were discovered by sages meditating upon the human fetus inside the womb. They observed the baby grows up around its mother's navel point, and that through the navel the fetus absorbs nutrients and expels waste. The fetus literally "breathes" through the umbilical cord from the mother into its own navel down to the perineum and up to the head and down from the tongue to the navel again. The navel point is thus said by Taoists to be the starting point for the flow of the primordial life energy, or "chi", and remains the point of strongest energy storage and circulation in the adult.

"Awaken Healing Energy Through The Tao" is a method for an adult to return to that state of dynamic energy circulation which existed inside the womb. In this sense this esoteric Taoist meditation is a rebirth process, a return to one's original, primordial self. What happened after birth that caused us to lose that original, perfect equilibrium that was so nurturing and permitted such healthy growth?

After a baby enters the world, his/her energy slowly "settles out" into hot and cold parts of the body. In the fetus this "yin" and "yang" energy was perfectly balanced in a kind of "lukewarm" mixture. But by the time a baby has grown to adulthood the hot or "yang" energy has gradually risen to the upper part of the body containing the vital organs such as the heart, liver, lungs and brain. The cold or "yin" energy has tended to settle in the legs, genitals, kidneys and lower abdomen.

As we age, the energy routes which bring vital power to our internal organs and enable them to function become progressively more blocked by physical and mental tension. The result is general fatigue, weakness, and poor health. A young person usually has sufficient energy to keep the routes less obstructed so that the power still flows. The organs are thus nourished, and there is little sickness. But if we do not live healthily and practice to keep the energy routes open, they will gradually close and cause emotional imbalances, premature sickness and old age.

The perfect energy circulation we enjoyed as babies was not yet impaired by the daily stress of living. Simply by re-establishing that same strong flow of "lukewarm" chi — mixed yin and yang energy — our vital organs will begin to glow with radiant health. When this healing power of the Tao — the life energy in its original, pure, undivided form — flows through our bodies, we regain the exuberant energy and rosy glow we once had as babies. Our true task is only to "re-awaken" this undivided healing power that was once an accepted fact in our being.

DIAGRAM 1
Energy enters the human fetus at the navel
and circulates in the Microcosmic orbit,
harmonizing yin and yang energy.

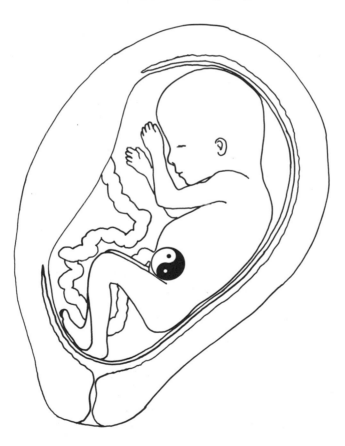

THE PRIMARY ENERGY CHANNELS

The nervous system in human beings is very complex and is capable of directing energy wherever it is needed. But the ancient Taoist masters discovered there are two primary energy channels that carry an especially strong current.

One channel they called the "Functional". It begins at the base of the trunk, midway between the testicles and the anus at a point called the perineum. It flows upward into the body past the penis, stomach organs, heart, and throat. The second channel, called the "Governor", starts in the same place. It flows from the perineum upwards into the tailbone and then up through the spine into the brain, and back down to the roof of the mouth.

The tongue is like a switch that connects these two currents, for when it is touched to the roof of the mouth just behind the front teeth, the energy flows in a circle up the spine and back down the front of the body. The two channels form a single circuit that the energy loops around in circles. When this energy flows in a loop around the body through these two channels, the Chinese masters said the "small heavenly cycle" or "microcosmic orbit" had been completed. Henceforth in this book we shall refer to this major energy loop as "the microcosmic orbit". Its vital current circulates past the major organs and nervous system of the body, giving cells the juice they need to grow, heal, and function.

PROPER WIRING OF THE ETHERIC BODY

The two main energy channels of the body can be compared to the main wiring of a house. Imagine a trunk line which brings power from outside into the building's service panel. This panel contains the circuit breakers that protect the inside wiring from short circuits and overloads. It also has the switches that control the current to all the rooms inside the house. This inside wiring is like the "six special power routes" in the body used in higher levels of Taoist meditation that branch off from the Microcosmic Orbit. In higher levels there are additional "wires" for especially heavy loads of energy that might surge into the system — the "thrusting route" in the middle of the body is one such wire.

Once your house, like your body, is properly wired and all the safety precautions have been made, it is ready to connect to the main utility company trunk line for power. You are ready to receive the power that comes from above and from beneath you without harm.

WHAT DOES IT MEAN TO "OPEN THE ROUTES"?

"Opening the routes" means clearing all obstructions that impede the flow of chi energy in their natural paths. Most obstructions take the form of physical, mental, or emotional tension. It helps to understand that these energy routes in the body are grounded in the larger balancing forces of nature which are exerting powerful influence over us at every moment. The healing power of natural forces can be tapped to help the body in clearing itself of the obstruction to its natural energy flow.

The route running down the front of the body (it may flow in an upward direction before the Microcosmic Orbit is linked together) the Functional Channel, has a yin, or cold nature. The route running up the back, the Governor Channel, is yang, or hot, in nature. The feet are said to be the ground or the "earthwire" and absorb negatively charged energy from the earth. The top of the head, or crown, is the "heavenly wire", or positive wire and absorbs the yang power from above, especially from the sun.

When these two routes are joined and cleared of obstruction the power will flow in a circuit between these two poles, positive and negative, linking the vital organs of the body to the main loop of the microcosmic orbit around the trunk and head of the body. So by simply opening the two main routes, Functional and Governor, a larger supply of warm "chi" current flows into every bodily organ. The process of mixing yin and yang, hot and cold, heaven and earth, takes place automatically, balancing your physical, mental and emotional selves.

LESSEN SIDE EFFECTS BY CAREFUL PREPAPARTION

Some meditation methods have the practitioner start by receiving power from above immediately. Only a few people —

those born with the proper channels already open and ready to use, and who have done nothing to cause them to be blocked — are capable of doing this immediately. Many people, including well known yogis, have damaged their organs with excessive heat or have released uncontrollable hallucinations by progressing before their bodies were prepared to handle high doses of raw energy.

The Taoist approach is more gradual. The practitioner makes use of higher energies by first clearing the routes and raising their level of "chi" production. When the two principal thoroughfares of the microcosmic orbit are opened, only then are the six additional special power routes opened, and more after that. This allows the body to absorb the natural forces flowing about us constantly like a sponge, and enables one to swiftly circulate the added vitality throughout the body. With all these routes open, every organ receives its full complement of energy and remains in harmony with the rest of the body system.

The warm current of "chi" helps wash away any blockage that might be present, massages the internal organs, and restores health to damaged and abused tissues. Many deadly diseases are prevented and the effects of stress and nervous tension are effectively flushed out of the system. Many practitioners open all the routes within a few months and learn to reduce leakage of their bodily energy to the point where an EEG records little or no energy waves.

ACUPUNCTURE AND THE MICROCOSMIC ORBIT

The Chinese sages studied the flow of energy from these two main channels, the Functional and Governor that connect to form the microcosmic orbit, and discovered other energy flow routes. It was along these energy meridians that the points used in acupuncture healing were also discovered. But before the art of acupuncture developed, using needles to impede or enhance energy flow along the various routes in an effort to restore normal function, the Chinese healers relied on circulating their energy internally in the microcosmic orbit to insure good health and long life. These masters of long life were much sought after, even besieged to teach the secret of living a long and harmonious life.

When acupuncture was first introduced it was considered an inferior form of medicine and was used mostly in extreme cases of sickness. The best doctors in China were the doctors who kept their patients from getting sick in the first place. The highest form of medicine was preventive. Today, while we are beginning to accept acupuncture as a reliable medical practice, we have yet to recognize our innate ability to prevent illness and heal ourselves using the energy flowing naturally through our bodies.

SUMMARY

In the Taoist system one begins by opening and completing two main channels, up the spine in back and down the front of the body. When linked together by the tongue on the roof of the mouth, these two routes form the Microcosmic Orbit and serve as a circulatory system for the body with built-in cooling safety valves.

Human energy tends to flow upward during meditation and may cause immense heat to accumulate in the brain coupled with bodily sensation, visual and auditory hallucinations, emotional outbursts, and various delusions. By completing up to a total of thirty-two routes (these smaller routes are not covered in this volume) the energy is well circulated, greatly reducing the overheating side effects of concentrated meditation and inducing relaxation.

Once all the energy channels are open, one can begin the practice of mixing and transforming the powers present in the various energy centers or chakras, a process known to the Taoists as "inner alchemy". Many formula are needed to bring about the proper effects and to harmonize the various energy systems of the body with the energy system of nature. As more power becomes available, the importance of opening the various routes becomes evident.

Without many clear and commodious channels to transport a considerable increase in energy, damage can result from an overload. These side effects range from the physical to the psychological and can be quite disturbing, even debilitating. If any side effects should ever occur, see the chapter on Safety Precautions and if necessary ask for advice immediately from a teacher of Taoist yoga. "Awaken Healing Energy Through The Tao" is a method evolved over many millenium to offer the practitioner the safest and most assured path to good health. If you proceed one step at a time up the ladder, you will be guaranteed success in reaching the top.

CHAPTER 2

PREPARE TO CIRCULATE
THE CHI ENERGY

1. CREATE A RELAXED ENVIRONMENT. The key to
Chi circulation is deep relaxation: in order to circulate the warm
current you must be calm within yourself. If you are distracted by
the television, passing cars, or your unmade bed, your mind will
turn outwards and you will be unable to focus on your energy. As
you progress you will learn to ignore the distractions and will be
able to meditate anywhere, but in the beginning choose a quiet
spot and a special time. The more comfortable the atmosphere the
more easily you can concentrate.

2. CLOTHES. During Chi (meditation) dress in loose-fitting
clothing. Loosen your belt and remove your glasses and watch.
Remember to keep the knees, nape of the neck and toes free of
binding clothing. Dress warmly enough so that you are not distracted by the cold.

3. ROOM. The room must be kept well-ventilated, but do not
sit in front of a window. The body generates excess heat during
meditation and a draft may cause a cold. Avoid meditating with
light shining in your eyes. If a room is too light it will disturb your
concentration; if too dark it may make you sleepy.

4. DIET. According to the Taoist masters, if you stop eating
when you are two-thirds full your stomach will have room to digest
the food. When you are too full you lose lucidity and power of
concentration.

Wait at least one hour after eating before meditating, and avoid eating cold foods including iced drinks and chilled fruit. They are extremely yin and tend to throw you out of balance. Let your foods warm up instead of eating them directly from the refrigerator. Your body saves energy by not having to heat the cold food.

You may attain a high plane of spiritual evolution without being a vegetarian. Both vegetarians and omnivores are subject to illness and decay. Simply eat whatever makes you feel best. Try to listen to your body's appetite and you will know what to eat. When you have an urge to eat something your body has a need for that food. Of course this applies only to those whose bodies are relatively healthy and have no extreme cravings for deadly substances such as refined sugar, salt, or oily food. If your health has been affected by perverted eating habits you will gradually recover a true sense of your nutritional needs by circulating the warm current of "chi" around your body. No one else can tell you what you need to attain inner harmony; vegetables alone will not make you pure or holier than fish. But you should try to eat food that is fresh and as free of chemical contaminants as possible.

5. STIMULATING THE FLOW OF CHI. To prepare for meditation first rub your face, ears, eyes, waist, and the soles of your feet. Rotate your head 12 times in both directions, then clasp your hands above your head and rotate your trunk 36 times in a circular motion.

DIAGRAM 2
Rub the soles of the feet to stimulate the flow of Chi.

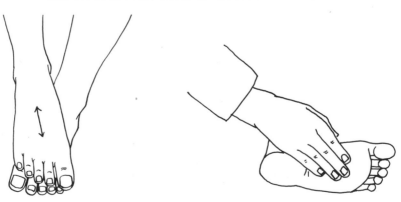

To prevent stiffness, promote flexibility, and insure an easier flow of energy upon awakening each morning, stretch your tendons, clench your teeth, and swallow your saliva. To stretch your tendons sit up with your legs extended out in front of you and grab your toes or ankles. Exhale completely and gradually bend at the waist stretching forward with your hands as far as you can go without straining. Practice nine times. Next beat your teeth together nine times then use your tongue to massage you gums. This will prevent gum disease and exercise your tongue. We deal with this more in the Chi Massage (Taoist Rejuvenation).

6. HOW TO SIT. Sit on the edge of a chair using your sitting-bones to find that delicate place of balance which will help hold you erect. Men should allow the scrotum to hang freely in the air; when the testes are freely suspended it is easier to draw in energy and awaken the sleeping giant within. The sitting position for women is the same except that if women sit in the nude or are scantily clad they should cover the genitalia to avoid energy loss. The back must be comfortably erect, the head bowed slightly forward, the feet firmly planted on the floor. The feet are the ground wire, and have ten channels of energy flow in each leg. In order to keep the energy flow fully in each leg, keep your legs in touch with the ground.

DIAGRAM 3

Incorrect sitting position   **Correct sitting position**

Sitting on a chair is the most comfortable way to practice the chi flow to the whole body. The feet are the root of our body so keep the energy flow to them and the hands resting on the lap with the right palm on top, clasping the left palm. This will complete the hand circle, and the energy will not leak out of the palm. The back should be quite straight at the waist though slightly bowed at the shoulders and neck. This minor forward curve of the upper back promotes perfect relaxation of the chest and allows the power to flow downward. In military posture, with the shoulders thrown back and the head held high, the power will lodge in the chest and fail to descend to the lower centers.

DIAGRAM 4
Both men and women place the right (Yang) palm
over the left palm (Yin),
to connect and seal the energy while meditating.

DIAGRAM 4A
The back should be straight.

7. HOW TO BREATHE. While concentrating the breath should be soft, long, and smooth. After a while you can forget about your breath. Attention to breath will only distract the mind which must focus on drawing energy to the desired points. There are thousands of esoteric breathing methods; you might spend your whole life mastering them and acquire no lasting energy.

DIAGRAM 5
To relax, practice taking long slow deep breaths
in the abdomen, not the chest.

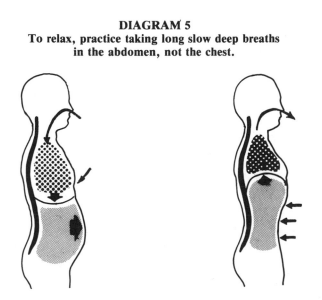

But once the Chi is awakened and you complete the route you may experience many different breathing patterns: rapid breathing, shallow breathing, deep breathing, prolonged retention of breath, spinal cord breathing, inner breathing, crown breathing, soles of the feet breathing, etc. You need not try to regulate your breath as breathing patterns will occur automatically according to the body's needs.

Breathe noiselessly through the nose. Make the breathing smooth and gentle. Any sound passage of the breath will mar your concentration, and if your breathing is rough you will not succeed in attaining a complete state of calm. But take care, if you interfere with the breathing you will arrest the flow of energy.

In the beginning if you have difficulty focusing, count from one to ten and ten to one, five times. You can take thirty-six abdominal long, slow, deep breaths which will lower the energy held in your chest, shoulders, arms, and head, and help you attain inner calm. Once you have acquired energy and concentration you can imagine energy entering every pore when you inhale and leaving every pore when you exhale. In this way you will experience the entire surface of your body breathing.

8. MENTAL ATTITUDE. Don't try to meditate when you are tired. If you are fatigued but still wish to practice, first take a stroll, a soothing bath, a short nap, or have a warm drink. Begin to practice when you feel refreshed.

Maintain a calm mind and an attitude of forgiveness. Be cheerful and remain open to life. Don't be consumed with ambition or worry. Your great task is to raise your consciousness and your capacity to love. Don't worry about tomorrow. Tomorrow will take care of itself. Happiness and a calm state are signs of spiritual progress.

Don't struggle. Don't try to force wandering thoughts out of your mind. Simply release your thoughts, watching as they depart. Imagine them as clouds dispersed by the wind. When they are gone the sun will shine through brightly. Detach yourself, be a spectator to the thinking process not a participant. Gradually you will learn to concentrate and direct the healing energy of the Tao.

9. POSITION OF THE TONGUE. The tongue is the bridge between the two channels, the Functional and the Governor. They

are separated by the tongue. There are three positions for the tongue. For the beginner, place the tongue where it is most comfortable. If it is uncomfortable to place the tongue to the palate, place it near the teeth. The correct place is called the "Heavenly Pool".

1. FIRST POSITION. The place near the teeth will produce air (wind) and will make it easy for you to fall asleep.

2. SECOND POSITION. The top of the palate before the soft-palate is the Fire Place. If touched for too long it will make the mouth and tongue feel dry.

DIAGRAM 6

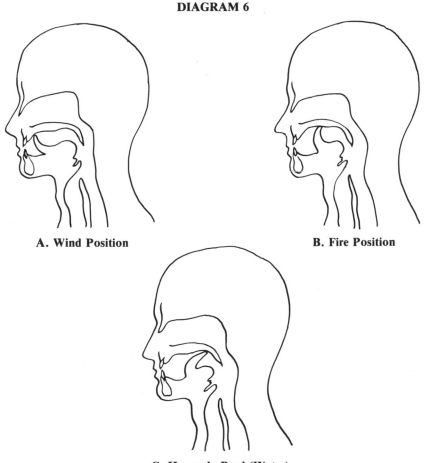

A. Wind Position   B. Fire Position

C. Heavenly Pool (Water)

3. THIRD POSITION. This is the Heavenly Pool position about 1½ inches in front of the teeth, stimulating the salivary gland that is under the tongue. The Heavenly Pool has two pools, which in the Tao system connect with the perineum Sperm Palace and the K1 Kidney, the Sole (Bubbling Spring). It connects with the kidney and runs up past the heart, so these two pools will stimulate the kidney and sperm energy to rise up past the heart and enter the small brain and the Pituitary Gland, which transforms it into brain energy. This will later on become Nectar and strengthen the heart energy.

CHAPTER 3

THE SECRET OF THE INNER SMILE

Once you've created a quiet, calming external atmosphere you must establish that same quiet and calm within yourself. If the room is conducive to meditating, but your jaw clenched, your neck stiff, shoulders tense, your back stiff, your stomach upset, you will not be able to circulate the chi energy and complete the microcosmic orbit.

A relaxed mental attitude and the thirty-six deep abdominal breaths will help to calm your mind and begin to relax your body. But to achieve full calmness means more than simply relaxing tense muscles and jittery nerves. To gain a deep and lasting state of relaxation requires that we develop a feeling of peace in our inner-most parts. Only when our vital organs like the heart, lungs, liver, kidney and stomach, nervous system and circulatory system are feeling relaxed, can we psychologically feel serene. To reach these organs, the ancient Taoist masters discovered a simple secret, the "inner smile".

THE HEALING POWER OF A SMILE

Have you ever walked down the street grumbling or worring about things you have to do, your relationships, your job, your whole life? When you glance up someone smiles at you, and before you know it you're smiling back. In only a split-second you've dropped your troubles, you stand up a little straighter, and walk on knowing everything is going to be okay. A genuine smile has tremendous power.

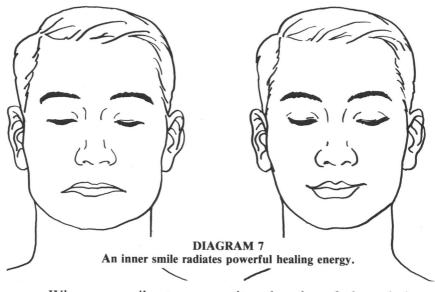

DIAGRAM 7
An inner smile radiates powerful healing energy.

When you smile at someone it makes them feel good about themselves. When you smile at your plants they feel your loving energy and they grow. When you go home, pat your dog on the head and smile at him, your dog will wag his tail to show you he's happy. But if you go home, yell at him and kick him, he'll cower, growl, or bite. If you scream at your loved ones they'll feel defensive and unloved.

A true smile is a sign of love, a transmitter of energy which has a warming, healing effect. It is a vehicle for music. A person who does not smile is like a guitar which is not played: the guitar sits in the corner, begins to warp, it's strings stretch out, and gradually the guitar cracks and decays. The non-smiler, likewise, does not develop his ability to give and receive love. His dark countenance and serious approach to life is often coupled with ulcers and other medical disorders as his life slowly crumbles for lack of care and love.

On the other hand, the guitar that is polished and played has its strings changed regularly, the bow adjusted and is kept safely in a case. A well-loved and tended guitar brings life and light to the musician, and often outlive its owner. The smiler, too, rings joy to people's lives, and leads a happy healthy life that may be soundly remembered long after physically passing away.

Unfortunately, while we all recognize the difference between cheery people and glum people, and while we associate happiness with health, and sadness with sickness, we still do not acknowledge the power of smiling or understand it's full potential. In short, we don't take smiling to our organs and nervous system seriously.

Why, for instance, if a smile is associated with health, aren't there doctors who specialize in smiling? If Saturday Review editor, Norman Cousins, used old Marx Brothers films to laugh away his rare connective disease, then why can't doctors and nurses use smiling energy to help heal their patients? Perhaps our hospitals should hire clowns and jesters to make their patients smile. More important, why hasn't smiling been used as preventive medicine? In smiling at our friends, families and loved ones, why have we not learned to smile to ourselves?

In ancient China, the Taoists taught that a constant inner smile, a smile to oneself, insured health, happiness, and longevity. Why? Smiling to yourself is like basking in love: you become your own best friend. Living with an inner smile is to live in harmony with yourself.

One look at our western society shows that we do not know the secret of smiling. The lack of harmony within ourselves is tragically apparent. We are plagued with an increase in physical and emotional illness that ranges from cancer to anorexia nervousa. Our loves are always shadowed by a world filled with violence and self-destruction. Both the individual and the collective society are threatened by rampant drug abuse and nuclear waste. Somehow, somewhere, we've lost sight of the Tao. We've broken the natural flow of life, and with it the power to heal ourselves.

SMILE LOVE INTO YOUR VITAL ORGANS

The complexity of global problems can be so overwhelming that most people simply give up trying to understand the whole picture of their life. Our heads reel from an overload of information that spews out from television, newspaper, radio and computers. The challenge is to simplify all this information into digestible form. This process of literally "digesting" reality is made difficult to the extent that we've separated our minds from our bodies.

If the body is healthy, it can easily assimilate the stress of modern living and even find it a creative challenge. But many people ignore their natural balancing mechanisms between the body and mind. They attempt to digest the world with their minds, piling up concepts, thoughts, and desires like giant mounds of mental baggage.

They ignore the fact that their body must carry this extra mental baggage around twenty-four hours a day, and eventually tires of the extra weight. Exhausted, the body gives up prematurely resulting in heart failure, stroke, arthritis, or liver dysfunction. The collapse is blamed on a poor physical body, but the overstressed mind is the true culprit.

Proof of our ignorance of the connection between body and mind is seen in the fact that most of us don't even know where our bodily organs are, much less their size, shape or functions. And if we happen to know intellectually, we still don't experience our organs in a tangible way because we ignore their constant subtle messages. For instance, we think we are satisfied when our mind is pleased: our intestines may be rebelling from over-eating, our lungs may be taxed by smoke, our kidneys may be overworked from coffee, but in our mind we've had a delicious meal, a good smoke, and a great cup of coffee. We are numb to our organ's feelings and thereby block what is potentially our deepest experience of good health.

We're like the irresponsible automobile owner who spends all his time waxing and polishing his car only to drive over bumpy, dusty roads. He avoids cleaning the spark plugs or changing the oil, then uses leaded instead of unleaded gasoline. When the car breaks down, he curses, complaining that he is not a mechanic, and then blames the car maufacturer when he's told the car needs a complete overhal.

We are really no different. We spend all our energy (and money) making certain our outer selves are presentable, then we abuse our inner selves by eating an imbalanced diet, drinking, smoking, and worst of all, denying ourselves love. And then we're shocked when out of the blue our lungs collapse, our kidneys fail, or we're told we have cancer.

Some people have an astonishing ability to convince themselves that their health is not caused by their own behavior, and quickly blame their illness on bad genes, old age, fate, etc. But most people are simply unaware that their illnesses are the direct result of accumulated years of stress and seemingly minor abuse of the physical body, especially of the vital organs. These vital organs are intimately connected to every aspect of our mind. Our body is the filter for all our perceptions, feelings, thoughts, as well as the storehouse for our memory, our very sense of identity.

Most people fail to realize that even if our mind temporarily stops functioning, if we cease to think or feel, our organs can continue to work. But the moment your spleen bursts, our heart stops, or your liver malfunctions, your life is in serious danger.

The brain is the boss, but organs do the work. Imagine your organs are working in a factory, your mind is the boss. If the boss is never around, or if he ignores the workers grievances (he's so concerned about his own affairs that he can't see that the workers have poor working conditions, they're overworked, and under paid) the workers will eventually become so discouraged and frustrated that they'll either go on strike or quit altogether. The factory shuts down, no goods are produced, and the boss is left trying to negotiate with the workers. But his power is diminished if the workers have already shut down the factory. It may never open again, and cause the boss to lose his livelihood. (Remember, the problem did not occur over night.)

HOW TO SMILE DOWN WITH THE INNER SMILE

START WITH THE EYES. To practice the inner smile begin by closing your eyes and smiling sincerely into them. Relax and feel a deep smile shining through your eyes. By relaxing your eyes you can calm your entire nervous system.

Your eyes are connected to your autonomic nervous system which is divided into two parts, the sympathetic and parasympathetic nervous systems. The sympathetic nervous system controls the flight or fight reaction. The parasympathetic permits the body to rest and feel secure. It generates calm, loving feelings and is in turn activated by similar feelings of love and acceptance from other people.

These two systems are linked with every organ and gland in the body. which are given commands through the nervous systems to speed up or slow down the activity of the body as needed. Thus it is through the link between your eyes and your nervous system that your entire range of emotions and immediate physical reactions are controlled. By relaxing your eyes with the inner smile, you free your mind of tension held throughout the entire body. The mind is then freed to concentrate and apply all its available creative energy to the task at hand, e.g. harmonizing itself with the environment. This connection between visual relaxation and the ability to concentrate is an essential Taoist insight.

After you feel your eyes tingling with a huge inner smile, direct that smiling energy down into your body and fill your vital organs with love. An easy way to remember the "smiling down" sequence is as follows:

> 1. THE FRONT LINE: Smile down into the eyes, face, neck, heart, and blood circulatory system, the lungs, liver, kidneys, adrenals, pancreas and spleen.
>
> 2. THE MIDDLE LINE: Smile down from the mouth to the stomach, small intestine, large intestine and rectum, simultaneously swallowing saliva.
>
> 3. THE BACK LINE: Smile down the inside of the vertebrae of your spine, one by one.

1. THE FRONT LINE. This smiling of chi energy from your eyes down your front through the organs will later aid you in circulating the microcosmic orbit. Your smile should flow effortlessly like a waterfall, from your eyes down through your vital organs towards your genitals. With practice your chi will flow through these organs automatically, helping them in their work.

2. JAWS. Smile down your face into your jaws. Your jaws are a major storehouse of tension. When you allow the energy created by that "inner smile" to go into your jaws you should feel your body letting up and tension releasing. This may be accompanied by tingling sensations or noises, so do not be alarmed should that happen.

3. TONGUE TO PALATE. The tongue is the bridge connecting the back (yang) and front (yin) channels. Place your tongue on the roof of your mouth just behind your front teeth. The correct position of the tongue is touching the soft palate in the rear of the mouth, but it is easier to leave it in front in the beginning. When chi flows into the tongue it may produce strange taste sensations and a warm tingle.

DIAGRAM 8
Front Line Smile:
the major vital organs

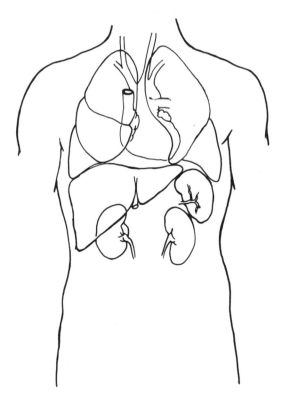

DIAGRAM 9
Middle Line Smile:
Swallow saliva to the
stomach and intestines.

DIAGRAM 10
Back Line Smile:
Begin at the eyes, then smile
down the inside of the spine,
vertebrae by vertebrae.

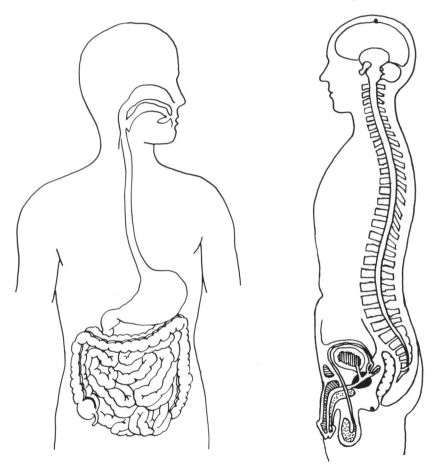

4. NECK AND THROAT. The neck region is another reservoir of tension. Contained in this area are many important nerves and blood vessels vitally important to your well being. The neck is the bridge between your brain and your body. If your neck is a traffic jam, knotted with tension and anxiety, the messages between your brain and organs will be confused and tense. If you cannot relax your neck you cannot complete the microcosmic orbit. Tighten your neck muscles then slowly allow them to relax.

Tuck in your chin and let your head sink into your chest. Ancient Taoists copied this technique from the behavior of the turtle. Relax the neck muscles by creating the illusion that they are no longer necessary to hold up your head. Smile into your neck and throat and feel the tension melt.

5. THE LOVING HEART. The heart pumps blood and chi energy through your veins and arteries. But in Taoist yoga the heart, along with the kidneys, is the main transformer of chi energy. This means that the heart is capable of both increasing your available chi and raising the quality of its energy to a more refined level.

The arteries are said to belong to yang energy and the veins to yin energy. The arteries therefore have a positive charge and the veins a negative one. When you smile and fill your heart with love you increase the rate of blood circulation and with it the exchange of yin and yang chi in the bloodstream. So smile into your heart and feel the loving energy of the smile spread throughout your circulatory system.

If you can use the smile and microcosmic orbit to aid the chi flow, the heart will work less. The smile from the eyes and the brain will help to circulate the chi energy and thus aid the blood to flow fully and freely while the heart relaxes. In conjunction with the proper diet and exercise, the likelihood of getting heart disease will be greatly reduced.

Feel the stream of relaxation flow down and spread from your face and neck into your heart. You will sense the heart to be cool and calm, and at the same time feel its physical substance. People who are nervous or who anger quickly often experience pain and tense feelings in and about the heart. Extending the smile relieves stored tension and enables a new kind of functioning to take place. Fill your heart with love. Let your heart be your "sweetheart".

6. LUNGS. Radiate the love in your heart to your lungs. Feel your lungs soften and breathe with a new ease. Feel the air inside lighten up as it enters and leaves the lungs. Feel their moist, spongy quality as you relax and fill your lungs with energy.

7. ABDOMEN. Now smile into your liver on the right side, just below the rib cage. If your liver is hard, if it is difficult to feel, soften it with your smile. Smile it back to life, rejuvenate it with your love.

Direct the smile to your two kidneys, in your lower back just below the rib cage on either side of the spine. The adrenal glands sit on top of them. Smile at your adrenals, and they may send you a burst of adrenalin. The kidney is the lower transformer of the veins and arteries. Smile to the kidneys and fill them with love. Like the heart, this will increase the flow of chi circulating through your system.

Allow the smile to flow throughout your central abdomen, through the pancreas and spleen. Then gently rest the smile in your navel. All of your organs can be "smiled to". If you are relaxed and happy and smile within, your organs produce a honey-like secretion. If you are frightened, nervous, or angry, they produce toxic substances instead. The process of smiling into the organs lightens their work load and enables them to function more efficiently. They have a hard job pumping and purifying hundreds of gallons of blood each day, breaking down raw food into digestible energy, cleansing toxic substances and storing our emotional tensions. By smiling into your organs you've made their day a cheerful one.

8. MIDDLE LINE: SWALLOW SALIVA INTO LOWER ABDOMEN. Smile once again in your eyes. Smile down into your mouth and swish your tongue around to collect saliva. When your mouth is filled with saliva, put the tip of your tongue to your palate, tighten your neck muscles, and swallow hard and quickly, making a gulping sound as you do. With your inner smile follow the saliva down your esophagus, through your internal tract and to your navel. Your saliva is a lubricating nectar that holds vital energy which is dispersed throughout the body from the navel center. Smile away the nervous energy in your stomach, and you will eat better food and find it easier to digest. Relax the smiling energy into your small intestine, large intestine, and rectum.

9. BACK LINE: SPINE. Now bring your focus back to your eyes. Smile into your eyes, your tongue, then begin to smile down the *inside* of your spinal column. Make sure your posture is straight with shoulders slightly rounded forward. Descend one vertebra at a time, smiling into each until you have reached the coccyx. The spinal column protects your central nervous system and is crucial in increasing your chi circulation. Starting from the

neck there are seven cervical vertebra, twelve thoracic vertebra, and five lumbar vertebra plus the sacrum and coccyx.

You should experience a feeling of great ease, warmth, and comfort in each vertebra. When the lumbar, coccyxal, and pubic areas are relaxed power is released and flows more easily up through the back.

10. END BY COLLECTING THE ENERGY AT THE NAVEL. With practice the entire smiling meditation can be done in just minutes, although at first it may take you longer to really feel the smile. When you end the meditation you do not want to have energy circulating around in the higher centers such as the head or the heart. The best place for energy storage in the body is the area of the navel, since it can easily handle the increased body heat. Most ill side effects of meditation are caused by excess energy in the head, but this is easily avoidable. (See chapter on Preventing Side Effects.)

To collect the energy simply concentrate your mind on your navel and imagine your energy spinning like a slow top inside, spiralling outward movement, inside your navel about one and a half inches deep, and 24 times back in to the navel. Men spiral first clockwise; women spiral counter clockwise. (put a watch at your naval to determine direction.) Then reverse and circulate the energy in the opposite direction.

IMPORTANT NOTE: You do NOT collect the energy at the navel after "smiling down" if you intend to immediately circulate chi in the microcosmic orbit as taught in the following chapter. You would circulate the orbit and then close by collecting the energy at the navel.

11. PRACTICE THE INNER SMILE IN DAILY LIFE. Although the inner smile is used primarily to help you to relax prior to practicing the microcosmic orbit, it is powerful as a meditation in its own right. Simply smiling the inner smile in your daily life can bring tremendous results. If you are constantly aware of your inner smile, it will transform your life.

One student went to ask her boss for a raise which she had been promised. She knew her boss was tight with money and would put up a fight, so she approached the grumpy boss with an inner smile as well as her outer smile. Such positivity reduced her boss' resistance, and they ended on good terms, with both of them smiling.

Another student's self-image changed radically from smiling down. Before his self-esteem was low, and he was continually fighting with himself, telling himself he wasn't up to par. After frequently practicing the inner smile he made good friends with himself, and began to realize potential hidden by his negative self-depreciations.

If you master an inner smile you may well feel like the turtle, entering the unknown sea with his protective shell snugly encased about him. Likewise, you will have the power to create a relaxed meditative environment capable of withstanding any external situation. Negativity will bounce off your smile and you will enjoy yourself wherever you are.

SUMMARY

The inner smile gives you love where you most need it, at home. Your home is your body because your body is where you live no matter where you are. Learn to see it as a community of many hardworking, devoted members who go unrecognized and are often abused. Learn to deal with your various parts as though they were your own children deserving of respect and affection.

Leave no one out and in no time you will know what it is to be loved and you will know what is meant by Loving Energy. Do this continuously and your world will blossom. The persons who "inhabit" your "inner" world, your vital organs, bones, blood, brain, etc., will afford you a new body and will enable you to relate to everyone and everything outside in a new, calm, loving way. So smile to yourself where ever you go, to who ever you see.

PART II:

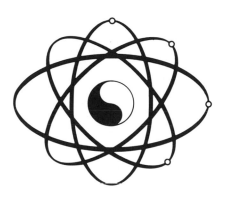

Circulate Healing Energy
In The Microcosmic Orbit

CHAPTER 4

BEGIN THE ORBIT: OPEN THE
FRONT CHANNEL, THE FUNCTIONAL

The functional channel (meridian) runs down the front of the body and is yin, female, or cold in quality; the governor channel at the back is yang, male, or hot. When joined, these two form the Microcosmic Orbit which links with all the vital organs of the body. By completing this route, the yin and yang mix in harmony, enabling you to increase your energy flow, and send energy, hormones, and vitality throughout your body. In this way energy can be collected, transformed and absorbed where necessary.

To establish the flow along the meridians some Taoists concentrated on easy-to-get energy points which were in accord with acupuncture points. By focusing on these specific power centers the Taoists realized that not only was chi released so that a warm current was felt, but that the energy points were activated, effecting a whole set of mental and physical functions. Focusing on the navel, for instance, effects the entire gastro-intestinal system, and the increased chi aids in digestion and balances the appetite.

The Microcosmic Orbit begins and ends at the navel, and the functional channel extends from the palate to the perineum. To open the front channel, we work from the navel to the perineum, and later, after opening the back channel, we open the remainder of the functional channel.

DIAGRAM 11
Points & Energy Centers

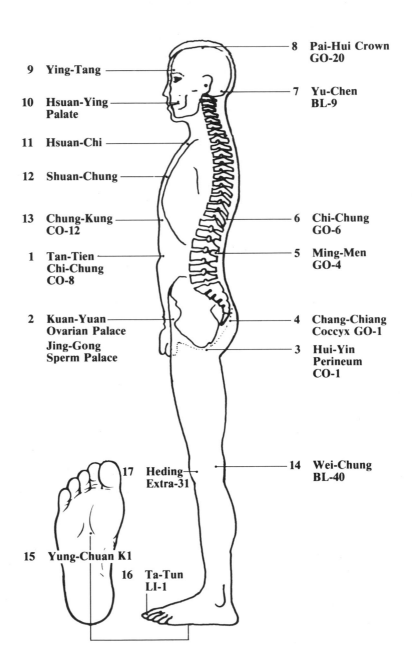

8 Pai-Hui Crown
GO-20

9 Ying-Tang

7 Yu-Chen
BL-9

10 Hsuan-Ying
Palate

11 Hsuan-Chi

12 Shuan-Chung

13 Chung-Kung
CO-12

6 Chi-Chung
GO-6

1 Tan-Tien
Chi-Chung
CO-8

5 Ming-Men
GO-4

2 Kuan-Yuan
Ovarian Palace
Jing-Gong
Sperm Palace

4 Chang-Chiang
Coccyx GO-1

3 Hui-Yin
Perineum
CO-1

14 Wei-Chung
BL-40

17 Heding
Extra-31

15 Yung-Chuan K1

16 Ta-Tun
LI-1

AWAKEN THE INDIVIDUAL HEALING POINTS

To awaken the energy in the individual points use your inner vision. Direct your vision inwardly to the point you wish to activate, and concentrate your mind on that point in your body. Do not create a visual image of the energy point in your mind. Rather bring your mind down from your head and put it in your body, e.g. your navel.

The energy, or chi flow that eventually results will be experienced differently by people depending on physical, emotional, and psychological conditions. Genetic make-up, past history, diet, immediate physical and mental stresses all contribute to the varying results. Some might feel the power of the warm current in a few minutes or a few weeks, while others may take months to feel it. Some experience the energy as hot or cold, some report tingling sensations and some see colors.

Many people experience soreness or pain when they practice, a sign that they are becoming sensitive to their formerly numbed body parts in the same way that we feel pain when our leg starts to come back to life after falling asleep. However you experience the energy is fine. Do not ignore the messages and sensations your body sends; if anything, listen more attentively and experience your body more fully. These messages are valuable signals that you are coming in tune with your etheric energy body that connects your physical body to your mind.

CHOOSING YOUR FIRST POINT: THE NAVEL

The first energy center is normally the navel, but it varies if you have problems such as high or low blood pressure, if you are old, or if you have chest problems.

The navel serves as the generator of electricity which supplies all the other points. The taoists considered the navel the earth or root of the body. It is the origin of energy: from the fertilized ovum the fetus is developed, linked to life by its umbilical cord. After birth the surrounding energy continues to enter through the same area.

The navel also is the place where breath originates. As blood and chi are drawn to this point a deep rhythmic breathing is established, and the entire mid-section of the body becomes a huge pump, vigorously circulating the chi and blood throughout the organism. This circulation distributes the life substances and relieves the heart of it's heavy burden.

Moreover, blood follows chi, and when vital power is distributed evenly throughout the body no energy accumulates at one point, thereby overheating or damaging the nearby vital organs. However, if one is injured or ill, energy can be directed to a particular site, concentrating all one's healing resource to the point where it is most needed. When the warm current has removed the impurities, the blood follows to finish the job of restoration.

USE A FINGER TO HELP CONCENTRATE

When you concentrate on the navel focus one and a half inches below the skin. In the beginning, apply pressure on the point with your index finger for one to five minutes, then return your hands to your lap with the right palm over the left. Concentrate on the sensation created by your finger, pressing again when the point becomes indistinct.

Once more, do not concentrate on breathing. Merely relax your eyes, tongue, and throat, and the mind will become still. Once the mind is calm the power will accumulate.

At first it is not easy to draw power to the energy center because your vital regenerative faculties have been abused for years. Your health cannot be restored overnight. The more you practice the stronger you will get, and you will be more able to endure heat produced by the higher voltage of chi.

If you have been concentrating on the navel for a long time but do not feel any energy, change your focus to the Ming-Men, the point opposite the navel on the spine. This helps the energy to rise up to the head and descend down the front of the body to the feet. However, if you do not feel anything in the navel but have definite signs of improved health, you are on the right track. Remember, the experience of chi is different for everybody. Some people experience warmth or bubbling sensations, others feel as though their navel area is expanding, and some people can increase their chi circulation without creating vivid sensations. No matter what your experience is, try to be as sensitive and aware of your body as possible. Adventure into your body, it is a vast land laden with riches.

HEART AND CHEST PROBLEMS

When some people concentrate on the navel too long, the energy moves up to the chest and effects the heart and lungs. If this happens the practitioner should either see a teacher, or choose a point lower down on the body so the energy in this problem area can drain out.

If, when concentrating on the navel, your pulse rate goes up uncomfortably, concentrate instead on the Ming-Men, the point opposite your navel in your lower back. If this doesn't help, and you are sweating profusely, shift your attention to the point between your eyebrows. If this causes too much pressure in your heart, bring your attention back to the Ming-Men.

NERVOUS TENSION, OLD AGE, PHYSICAL WEAKNESS

If you have nervous tension concentrate on the navel, alternating with the Ming-Men (opposite the navel on the back). If you are older or physically weak, concentrate on the Yin-Tang (point between the eyebrows).

HIGH BLOOD PRESSURE

For high blood pressure first focus on the navel, then bring your attention to the feet. In the beginning you can tape two prickly nuts over the Yung-Chuan points (Bubbling Spring) on the balls of your feet. The sensation of the nuts pressing into your feet will help to keep your attention in your feet. By focusing on your feet you put your mind into your feet, which directs the energy and blood there, consequently lowering your overall blood pressure. Do not focus on the Yin-Tang (mid-eyebrow) or Pai-Hui (crown of head) because it will cause a great deal of blood and chi to go to the head, further raising the blood pressure.

DIAGRAM 12
To lower high blood pressure,
concentrate on Yung-Chuan in the
center of the sole of the foot.

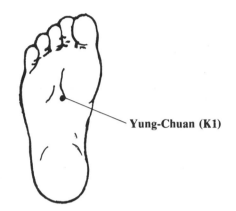

Yung-Chuan (K1)

One 55 year old student had blood pressure that stayed at 150/100, even though he took pills morning and evening. After completing the routes and concentrating for about 5 months his blood pressure came down to 135/90 (he continued to take pills). After that he was unable to sleep for ten days. After discussing the situation with his doctor, the doctor reduced the dosage of medicine to half because the student's blood pressure seemed controlled. After cutting the dosage he was able to sleep again and his blood pressure stayed at 135/85.

If you have high blood pressure, find a physician who would be interested in using concentration to help control your blood pressure. He should check your blood pressure regularly to see if the chi circulation is effective for you.

LOW BLOOD PRESSURE

Concentrating in the mid-eyebrow region will enable power and blood to flow into the head, aiding low blood pressure. But like those with high blood pressure, those with low blood pressure should have it checked regularly. Once the blood pressure has returned to normal you should concentrate at the navel for fifteen minutes then shift the power up to the head for fifteen minutes.

DIAGRAM 13
A. For low blood pressure, begin by
concentrating between the eyebrows.

B. For abnormally low blood pressure,
begin by concentrating at
the crown of the head.

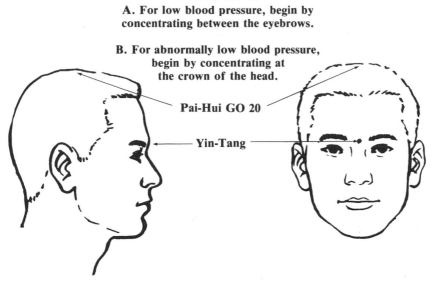

Pai-Hui GO 20

Yin-Tang

While the navel is a good starting point for most people who
are healthy, those who have high blood pressure or stomach and
intestinal problems, it is not good for those with low blood pressure because it causes the blood to drop.

GASTRO-INTESTINAL PROBLEMS

Anyone with gastro-intestinal problems will have more difficulty in opening the meridian because the digestive organs are linked to it. Each of these organs must be cleansed and strengthened
before the route may be completed. Your digestion and
elimination will greatly improve during your work on the Functional Channel.

Remember that once you complete the Microcosmic Orbit
and are able to collect more power you will be able to cure yourself. You will be able to bring your life force to the afflicted area.

It is important not to think of your self as sick or weak. You
can be free of an ailment no matter how long you may have had it.
Very often the difference depends on your attitude. The psychosomatic origin of illness is widely known. If you have confidence in
this method, your psychosomatic ailments will be banished. In ef-

fect, you will be overcoming your hidden desire for illness that first made you ill. The increased circulation of chi between your mind and your body will cause these hidden negative desires to surface and dissipate.

When the Ching-Chi Sperm energy first awakens, you may have difficulty telling whether it is real or imagined. But soon you will be absolutely convinced of the indisputable reality of the energy flow. It will start in the abdomen or the hands or legs or the big toes. Those who run or practice Tai Chi or Kung Fu often feel it first in the legs. Those who use their hands much will often feel it there first. A warm feeling of waves or bubbles is described as arising in the abdomen. Though everyone is altogether unique in this regard, the sensations are not to be imagined, however, because they are not like anything one has already experienced.

DIAGRAM 14
The First Energy Center
Meditating on the navel point
strengthens the Gastro-Intestinal organs.

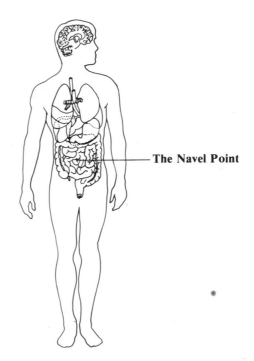

The Navel Point

DIAGRAM 15
The Second Energy Center
**For men, the Sperm Palace is located 1½ inches
from the base of the penis.**

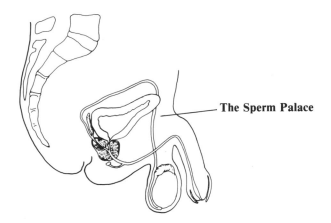

The Sperm Palace

THE SECOND ENERGY CENTER:
FOR WOMEN, KUAN-YUAN (OVARIAN PALACE)

The second energy center is in the Kuan-Yuan, the mid-point of the ovaries. To locate the point place your hand flat on your stomach with your thumbs at your navel. Directly below your pinky, in a straight line from the navel is the mid-point, 1½ inches in from the skin. In later practice this point becomes a great source of energy.

THE SECOND ENERGY CENTER:
FOR MEN, JING GONG (SPERM PALACE)

The second energy center is located in the Sperm Palace, the area of the prostrate gland and seminal vesicles in the lower abdomen just above the penis.

Before concentrating you can use your index fingers to apply pressure to the area for one minute, returning your hands to your lap and concentrating on the sensations. Apply pressure again as the feelings fade.

FOR UNMARRIED AND YOUNG MEN

The sperm palace is important for a man because it can cause him to be sexually aroused. If this happens, bring the power back from the Sperm Palace to the Ming-Men (point opposite the navel on lower back). This sexual energy can be used to greatly increase the circulating power of your chi, but first you must learn to circulate the Microcosmic Orbit without sexual distractions.

FOR MIDDLE-AGED AND OLD MEN

Those who feel less sexual stimulation and older people, 40 to 60 years old, can concentrate on the sperm palace until they feel power. If, however, they begin to have night emissions, they should also switch to the Ming-Men.

Those who do not have this problem can concentrate at the Sperm Palace until they experience warmth and a feeling of lightness in the area. If they have any kind of sensation other than what they normally experience in their meditation, they can shift their attention down to the Hui-Yin (perineum), midway between the anus and penis or vagina.

THE THIRD ENERGY CENTER:
HUI-YIN OR PERINEUM

The Hui-yin or Gate of Life and Death is found in the lower part of the trunk amidst the endings of many blood vessels and nerve endings. It is located at the mid-point between the anus and the penis or the vagina. Because it is lower, it tends to lose power. You can help stimulate this point by rubbing it until you feel it is warm. This area is very tender and you must remember not to rub too hard.

When you concentrate on the Hui-Yin, the time needed to collect and awaken the power is different in each person due to differences in genetic make-up. Some might take long, some might not. But, on the average, it should take two to four weeks if you practice twice a day for 15 to 30 minutes at a time.

If you still don't feel anything by then, you can extend the time for up to four weeks. You should not persist any longer than that. Move on to the next point, otherwise you might get congestion in your chest and/or heart pain. If this happens, it means that you have developed and collected too much power in that area. Instead of the power having travelled down to the base of the spine, it has gone up to the chest. Shifting your concentration to the Ming-men solves the problem and you will be symptom-free in a few days.

DIAGRAM 16
The Third Energy Center

For both men and women
the Hui-Yin (perineum) is
located midway between the anus and genitals.

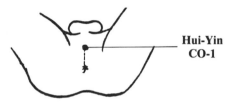

Hui-Yin
CO-1

Concentrating on this point sometimes leads to vibrating sensations or the feeling that something is jumping inside or a strong sexual arousal. Abdominal breathing can cause an erection to recede and allows for the concentration to continue without interruption. If you concentrate on this point too long however, it can open the thrusting routes (or Kundalini), which leads to various side effects. If the energy succeeds in passing very quickly up through the throat chakra and continues up to the top of the head to the crown, where it spreads out sprinkler-like, showering down over the practitioner, there will be very few, if any side effects. In fact if you have managed to open all the channels, your whole system will be nourished in the process.

Time is essential in all meditation. You cannot expect any results without putting in a great deal of effort. Remember that the navel is the generator and every time you commence practicing you have to start from this point. When you feel power has developed there (warmth, tightness, expansion, etc.), bring it down to the second point, then down to the third.

CHAPTER 5

OPEN THE BACK CHANNEL:
THE GOVERNOR

From the Hui-yin the energy moves to the Chang-chiang, or sacrum, and begins its ascent up the back to the crown of the head and the brow point. The back channel is extremely important as it contains two pumps, one at the sacrum (the large bone at the lower end of the spine), the other at the Yu-chen (back of the neck near the upper end of the spine).

The first pump sends chi and spinal fluid up to the neck, the second receives the chi and spinal fluid and pumps it up into the brain. Opening the back channel is like bringing fresh air to a stuffy room. Your spinal column and head will be refreshed, the nerves will be activated, and the extra oxygen and blood flowing to your brain will make you feel more alert, more alive.

THE FOURTH ENERGY CENTER: CHANG-CHIANG/ (COCCYX)

The fourth energy center point is the Chang-Chiang (Woii Lui) at the coccyx. This point is very important because it is here that the power is either returned to the body or lost. When the generative power (sperm power) is returned, it passes through this canal and into the spinal cord and then to the brain. This has been called the Passage to the Door of Life and Death because it is here that the "warm current" is said to enter the central nervous system.

DIAGRAM 17
Energy flows upward through the
major points of the Back Channel.
(Governor Meridian)

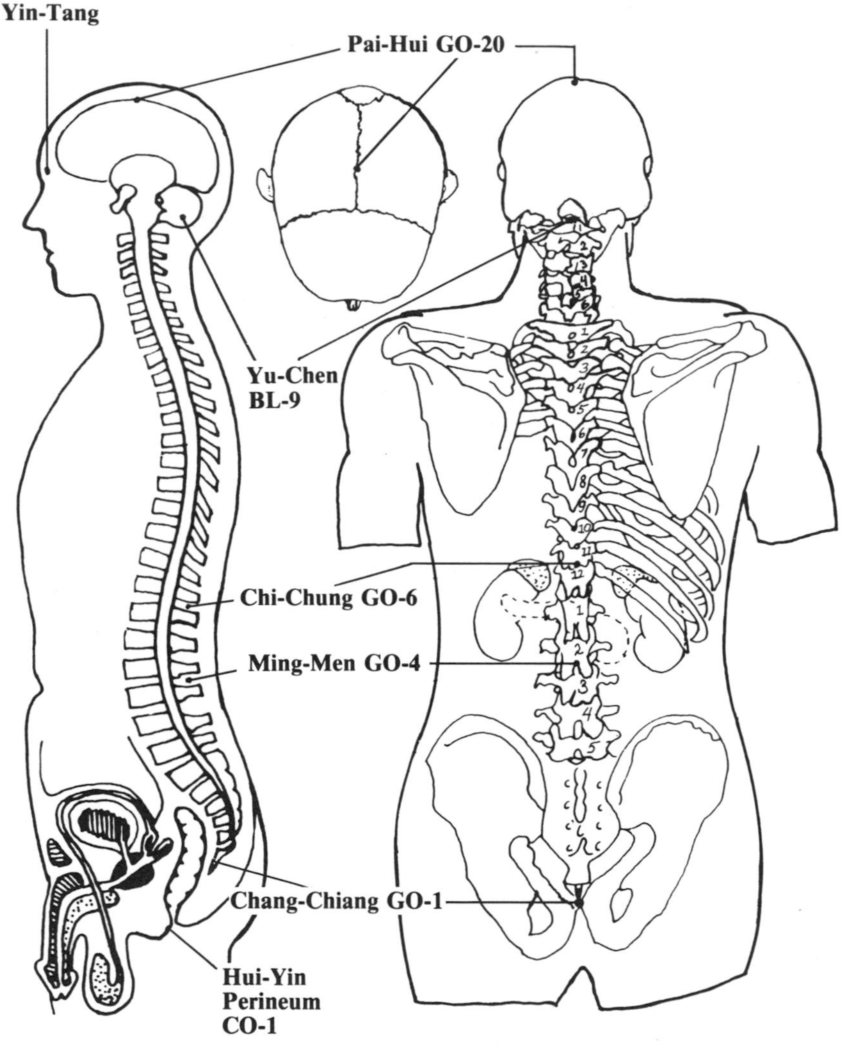

Yin-Tang

Pai-Hui GO-20

Yu-Chen
BL-9

Chi-Chung GO-6

Ming-Men GO-4

Chang-Chiang GO-1

Hui-Yin
Perineum
CO-1

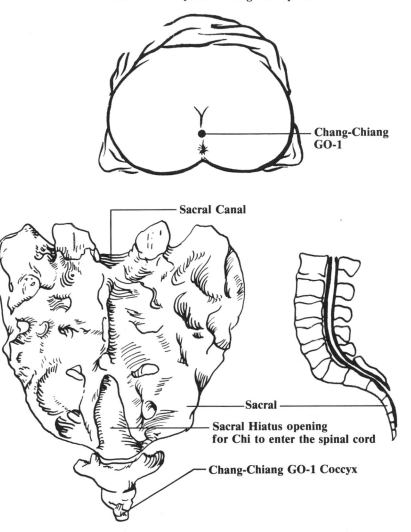

DIAGRAM 18
At the Fourth Energy Center, (Chang-Chiang)
the coccyx, sexual energy enters the
central nervous system through the spine.

Chang-Chiang
GO-1

Sacral Canal

Sacral

Sacral Hiatus opening
for Chi to enter the spinal cord

Chang-Chiang GO-1 Coccyx

When you have concentrated for some time you may feel a sensation of warmth and pressure rise up into the coccyx through the many nerve endings and the eight holes, which in the esoteric system are called the holes of the soul. The first level, opening the

Microcosmic Orbit, may be said to be the preparation of the way. The energy that passes here is the real sperm and ovary power and is the energy of the life force that is produced in the body and cells. The second level trains the chi to move along 34 additional routes and involves the cleaning of the organs. In the third level sperm or ovary power is awakened and transformed into a higher level of "chi power". This "power" pushes its way upward in through the coccyx. At that time some people may feel a needle-like pain. Some may report having a feeling of tightness there and others will be aware of something pushing its way inside. With continued practice the "power" or "warm current" pushes higher and higher. It will help you to open the point much more easily if you rub the coccyx with a soft cloth until you feel warmth there and then sit down to practice concentration.

DIAGRAM 19
The Fifth energy center Ming-Men (GO 4),
is a safety valve
to cool excess Yang energy in the head.

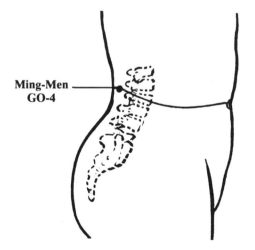

Ming-Men
GO-4

THE FIFTH ENERGY CENTER: MING-MEN
(OPPOSITE NAVEL POINT ON SPINE)

This point is the Ming-men, the Door of Life. It is the mid-point of the kidney, between L2 and L3 on the vertebrae. It is at this point that kidney power is concentrated. The left kidney is Yin and the right is Yang and at the center point is a balance between the two. The Ming-men (the main power point of the body) then, is the harmony point, containing Yin power. When you concentrate here, the power rises up the back or descends to the feet. This helps to prevent some of the side effects that occur when the power may suddenly surge up to the head. Those are standing, sitting, or walking, can use the Ming-men as their point of concentration.

BACK PAIN WHILE CONCENTRATING

Those of you who have back pain may find that the pains intensify when you concentrate on the Ming-men. Do not let that stop you. Before concentrating rub your hands together to produce warmth and place them on the painful area. When you first start Ming-men practice it might help to use scotch tape to fasten something prickly over the point or press the point for about a minute before concentrating on it. In time you will need only a few minutes to concentrate and collect energy. Many people feel the power more readily at the Ming-men than at the navel.

IMPORTANT NOTE: Try to remember when you concentrate, to let the power (warm current) flow. Do not try to direct the power. In the beginning, when you feel warmth in the navel, move your point of concentration down. The power follows this shift of attention, it is not that you have brought the power down. The power in your body knows where to go.

THE SIXTH ENERGY CENTER: CHI-CHUNG (OPPOSITE THE SOLAR PLEXUS ON THE SPINE)

The sixth energy center is located between the adrenal glands (T11), opposite the solar plexus on the spine.

The adrenals stimulate the inner part of the medulla in the brain, which prepares the organism for fight or flight. The outer part, the cortex, governs sodium balance and is involved in blood sugar level. Those who have diabetes may find that concentration on this point will help them to lower their blood sugar level. Allergy sufferers may also find relief by concentrating here.

If you are weak or ill, you can concentrate on this point any time. This practice can be very stimulating. Young people and those who are stronger, should not focus on the Chi-chung in the evening because it will keep them awake.

STIMULATE THE PANCREAS

When you concentrate on the Chi-chung (adrenal gland), you also activate or stimulate the pancreas. Like the adrenal glands, the pancreas is involved in blood sugar level and concentration on this point may have a normalizing effect. Whether this can help those who have diabetes would have to be born out by extended tests with many subjects under controlled conditions for a considerable period of time. However, without doubt, there would be improvement in the condition. As you continue concentrating on this point the power will collect and gradually push its way up to your head. The power of this point is the mixture of that found at the navel (point no. 3), the coccyx body (point no. 4) and the harmony of the kidney power (point no. 5).

THE SEVENTH ENERGY CENTER: YU-CHEN/ BACK OF THE NECK

The Yu-chen is the cerebellum. This part of the brain controls breathing, heartbeat, and various functions associated with the automatic nervous system. Thus, when the chi passes up the back to the Yu-chen point many changes will occur. Many different kinds of breathing patterns become available and are activated naturally according to necessity.

SHOULDER AND UPPER BACK PAIN

Those people who have shoulder and/or upper back pains may find that the power will not be able to flow beyond those areas or, at least will be slowed so that it takes much longer for it to reach the head. With continued practice many people have found that their back problems have been alleviated and even cured as the power works its way through on its upward path.

However, if the power builds up in the brain you may experience pain, nausea, illusions, irritability, insomnia, mood swings, and sleepiness. Be sure to direct the power down to your navel when you finish your practice period.

THE EIGHTH ENERGY CENTER: PAI-HUI/ CROWN OF THE HEAD

The Pai-hui (Niwan) is called the crown or the pineal body and is located above the mid-brain. Its functions are related to sensitivity and to the sexual cycle. It governs the hindbrain, hearing, body rhythm, equilibrium, perception of light through the eyes and skin, and is the superior counter-support of the brain and spinal cord. In Chinese it is called the Hundred Point Joint or the compass of men, because it is at the top of the crown of the head. When you concentrate here you may feel pressure or a sense of expansion in the middle of the head. This is an indication of power flow. When this happens, concentrate on the next point and remember not to spend more than a month practicing on any one energy center.

When the power passes through the mid-brain and the region of the pineal gland, you may feel some tightness or a kind of pressure pushing forward and backward in this area. You may also suddenly feel very sleepy. When the power freely passes through this point you will be afflicted less by illusion, you will be able to concentrate better, and your head will feel much lighter. However, as blood flow to the head increases, your eyes may redden. When the power builds up more some people may see light, a rainbow of colors, the sun, the moon, or a star twinkling before their eyes. Others may feel that they can foresee the future (but that is an illusion because occult vision is still far off at this stage). No matter what comes up, simply find ways to calm your mind.

Completing the Microcosmic Orbit does not mean that some special sense will be opened to you, though the energy or chi vibrating in the brain and coursing back and forth through the nervous system can lead to various aberrations of the senses. You may see and hear many unusual things, but all of them will simply be illusions, so try to ignore them.

Some practitioners describe being surrounded by light. Traditional Chinese masters would explain such an experience as being due to some physical ailment which gradually reflects outwardly. Those who have weak kidneys or a low sex drive will reflect a black light. Those with liver illness find that the light that is reflected is green. People with heart disease report seeing red light. Lung disease is expressed as a white light. Spleen and stomach illness is indicated in yellow and for those with gall bladder disease, the light which is reflected will be black. If the redness of the eyes does not go away after practicing for two or three hours, you should consult a doctor.

THE NINTH ENERGY CENTER: YIN-TANG/BROW POINT BETWEEN EYES

The Yin-tang is the pituitary gland and is called the "Tsu Chiao" or the Original Cavity of the Spirit by Taoists. In fact, there are many names for it in the Taoist Encyclopedia (Life Palace, Yu Ting, Jade Cauldron, etc.). This point is located between the eyebrows, above the nasal cavity. It is the master endocrine control gland, regulating growth, gonadal function, the adrenals and the thyroid.

It is said to govern the forebrain, vision, the right eye, as well as being the seat of love, compassion, knowledge, integration or personality, love of humanity and devotion. It is further said to be the seat of intelligence, conceptual memory (reading, thinking, studying), linear sequential time consciousness, abstract and conceptual thinking, compulsiveness, racism, sexism and paranoia.

This pituitary and the pineal gland are extremely important when completing the routes, for it is at these two points that you can check your power flow. When you concentrate on the navel and store power there, energy suddenly rises up and passes through the Niwan (the pineal gland). The next checking point is the Yin Tang (the pituitary gland). When you have completed the Microcosmic Orbit you can use these two, the Niwan and the Yin-tang, to see whether indeed there is a power flow. The rest of the points are usually not sensitive enough for this. To complete the route, the power has to flow down from the soft palate, through the tongue, into and through the throat, the Hsuan-chi, the

Shuan-chung (heart chakra) the Chung-wan (solar plexus) and finally the navel again.

When the power has passed from the midbrain to the fore-brain and then to the pituitary gland and the mammalary bodies, many students will feel pressure in both the left and right sides of their forehead, which is due to resistance to the flow often found when the route narrows as it comes down through the nose. This may stimulate the release of mucous or even lead to sinus trouble, if you are inclined that way.

After some time you may experience a fragrance. This is said to be caused by hormone glands purifying the internal organs. The aromas vary from person to person and also depends upon the degree of one's development. It is impossible to describe all the various senses that have been reported but flowers, perfumes, wine bouquet and coconut water have been mentioned. Along with the fragrance, there may be needle-like sensations or a feeling as if something were pressing down on one's forehead or hammering in the middle of one's head. This is again due to the fact that there is reesistance to the flow of energy. If you can ignore these feelings, the condition will gradually abate.

Concentrating on the brow point reduces the jarring effects of sudden loud noises. By contrast, students who concentrate on the navel do not have this facility. A degree of stability is reached, then, by the time you reach the point between the eyebrows. The tendency to worry will diminish and disappear as practice progresses. From then on you feel more saliva being released, which is said to be caused by hormones which are activated in the pituitary gland. With continued practice, the saliva will become more sweet and fragrant, at which time it is referred to as nectar.

This nectar helps to stimulate appetite and to activate all of your bodily systems. When your appetite is good, your digestion and assimilation are improved and you feel both content and invigorated. To top it all, you will also feel very calm. Students at this level report that they hear internal noises ranging from the beating of the heart and the magnified sound of their breathing to the rushing sound of the blood as it passes through blood vessels and the workings of their various inner organs. They even describe sounds, which Indian Yogis have for centuries referred to as divine. Most of these smells and sounds have always been there, but have been overshadowed by our attention to other things. As you grow quieter, and become less distracted, these ever present sounds become evident with the exception of the nadis, the divine sounds, which alter characteristically as one progresses spiritually.

When you have finally reached the point between your eyebrows, you are half-way finished. This doesn't only refer to opening the Microcosmic Orbit and other routes, but to what follows as well. The next stage (after the routes have been opened) involves the transportation of vital materials, the hormones as well as chi in the practical application to one's daily life of these new found abilities. These steps have already been described as organ purification, stimulation and development of the vital flow for the healing of illness. It brings strength and vitality to those who have been weak and finally rejuvenation and long life.

This calls for a very subtle balancing of powers and methods of approach to avoid the many pitfalls that side-effects can bring. The danger here is real. Without the proper knowledge as to how to proceed, outright physical and emotional damage can result. Some of the side-effects, again, are sensations of tightness or heaviness in the head, sleepiness, ear-noises, toothaches, sinusitis, nervousness, anger and irritability, all of which are due to having too much power accumulated in the head. The precaution, again as a reminder, is to be sure to bring the power back down along the route it travelled on its way to the head and/or being sure to end each practice period by returning it back to the navel in the prescribed manner. At the navel circulate the chi clockwise (if you are male) 36 times and then counterclockwise 24 times, ending by pushing in at the navel (reversing the direction of circling if you are female).

If you concentrate solely on the forehead or if you do so for long periods of time without having properly opened the routes, you will have most of these ill effects. Of the hundreds of students I have taught, most of them have reached higher levels of practice without much, if any, such trouble. Our aim here is to acquaint you with the side effects that can occur and how to prevent them so that you can be alerted to what can happen as you practice and thereby be more successful in your endeavors. Younger people, who have stronger power, must be more careful and should be sure to bring the power down to the navel at the end of each session.

CHAPTER 6

COMPLETE THE MICROCOSMIC ORBIT

When the energy reaches the area of the eyebrows it either pushes up out of the top of the head, leaks out the ears or eyes, or comes down the front of the body towards the navel. Pushing up through the top of the head requires that the bones be cracked apart, which takes tremendous power. It is much easier to push down through the palate and complete the route.

BEGINNERS: REVERSE THE CHI FLOW

Easiest of all, however, and most recommended for beginners who are often unable to send the energy through the palate, is to return the energy to the navel along the same route it came from. Simply reverse the flow of the chi and take it back down the spine and continue all the way to the feet. Then bring it up your front to the navel, throat, and palate.

Practice the following sequence to drain excess energy collected in the head and circulate it to the Door of Life and the soles of the feet.

1. From the area between the eyebrows direct the warm current down to the nose for about 10 minutes and then bring the energy down even lower. With practice, you will develop the ability to direct this force so that it will flow as you will it to.

2. Bring the power back up to the Pai-Hui (crown of head).

Stop for a while, allowing the power to flow backward from the mid-eye region to the Yu-Chen (back of neck).

3. Pause there for a while and then proceed down to the Ja-Jie, which is at mid-shoulder level and from there down to the Chi-Chung (T11) and then the Ming-men (L2 and L3) in the back and opposite to the navel. Stop and concentrate here longer until you feel tense in your forehead.

DIAGRAM 20
The Small Heavenly Cycle (Microcosmic Orbit)

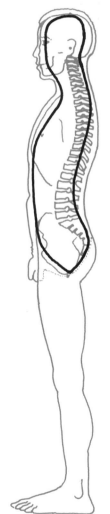

4. Then shift your attention down to the coccyx and then to the Hui-Yin in the perineum (mid-point between the anus and the penis).

5. This route then divides into two, one through each leg, descending down, along the inside of the thighs down to the inside of the ankle (the inside regarded as the Yin Power) and ending in the soles of the feet at the Yung Chuan (K1). You should then concentrate here (at the Yung Chuan) until you feel it become warm. When you first begin this practice you might try taping a prickly nut to the bottoms of your feet, so that when you step on it as you walk the energy center there will be activated. In time, energy will emanate as a warm, tingly feeling and spread out through your feet and legs.

6. Raise the energy up the front up to the big toes, stop for a while, then go to the knee and then up the leg to the perineum.

7. Proceed to the navel point. Pause and gather additional chi.

8. Raise the chi up to the heart, the throat and into the tongue that is pressed against the palate. Eventually the chi will connect with the point above, Yin-Tang, the brow, thereby completing the Microcosmic Orbit.

DIAGRAM 21
Use the tongue to link the flow of energy
between the front and back channels,
through the palate.

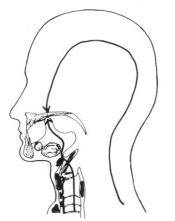

THE TENTH ENERGY CENTER:
TONGUE TO THE PALATE

Students who initially have great success in circulating chi power with no ill side effects may choose to proceed directly in joining the front and back channels. This involves lowering the energy from the Yin-Tang, or brow point, to the next energy point, the palate.

Other beginning practitioners should wait until they can easily return the energy by the reverse route down the spine/leg and up to the navel/palate before trying to connect the brow point and palate directly from above.

Even though the palate is constructed of soft bone it takes a considerable period of sustained effort for most practitioners to penetrate it and complete the route. The force which is generated in this practice often causes side effects such as headaches, illusions, erratic mood swings, insomnia, irritability and vague aches and pains. If such effects persist, immediately reverse your chi flow back down the spine to the feet. Also, read the chapter on "How to Prevent Side Effects".

In the beginning, place the tip of your tongue just behind your front teeth (later you will transmit more energy if you place it in the middle of the soft palate or even further back along the roof of the mouth). The palate links the front and back channels, and the tongue on the palate links the switch that enables the energy to flow in a complete circuit. If you watch sleeping babies you will see

DIAGRAM 22
Energy Flows Through
the Palate During The
Microcosmic Orbit

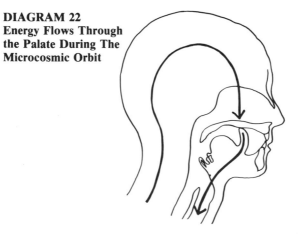

that often they keep their tongue on the roof of their mouths. They know instinctively how to circulate the microcosmic orbit as their yin and yang energy is still naturally balanced. Even thumb sucking may be an attempt to connect the channels!

When you put yur tongue to your palate you may feel sensations, or you may feel nothing. If you feel a small vibration, or your tongue moves back and forth involuntarily, chances are you have completed the orbit. Some people, however, do not feel sensations. If you do not feel sensation, but your health has improved, and you feel lighter, less worried, and more energetic, you probably completed the orbit.

THE ELEVENTH ENERGY CENTER: HSUAN-CHI (THROAT)

The Hsuan-Chi is the energy center of the thyroid and parathyroid glands. Concentrating here will often cause coughing or difficulty in breathing. When the energy pushes up through the throat and enters the mouth some people have been known to cough up dark, sticky mucous. This is considered to be

DIAGRAM 23
**The throat, heart and solar plexus comprise
the 11th, 12th and 13th energy centers.**

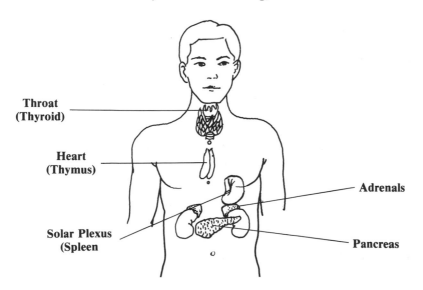

Throat
(Thyroid)

Heart
(Thymus)

Adrenals

Solar Plexus
(Spleen

Pancreas

characteristic of the clearing of this energy center and this leads to a free flow of energy from the throat to the tongue. Most people feel more calm and less worried when this energy flows from the navel up to the throat and to the tongue and with no congestion in the chest. They are simply freed of stress in opening the route. It does not mean that they will never have any worries or anxiety but that they will feel more calm and will be able to sit and concentrate more easily.

In this level we are linking all the energy centers together; not opening or cultivating the center (chakra) of the Microcosmic Orbit.

THE TWELFTH ENERGY CENTER: SHUN-CHUNG (HEART)

The heart center, the center for rejuvenation, for love and joy, is located mid-way between the nipples at the thymus gland, is an extremely vital point that is easy for most people to focus on. This will be dealt with extensively on the fifth level of the Tao Esoteric Meditation. Concentrating here very quickly leads to great stores of energy, and so many people tend to concentrate longer on this point. You must exercise caution, for when you collect heat and concentrate here too long, the energy is reab- sorbed in the pericardium (a fibro-serous sac which surrounds the heart to beat faster. As a result there will be difficulty in breathing and pain in the chest on the upper left side and in the sternum.

Do not concentrate here too long when you feel warmth or feel your chest extended.

THE THIRTEENTH ENERGY CENTER: CHUN-KUNG (SOLAR PLEXUS)

Half-way between your sternum and your navel you will find your solar plexus. This area is the frontal site of many power centers (spleen, adrenal, pancreas, and stomach). People who have stomach or digestive problems will find themselves belching frequently and passing wind. This is not cause for alarm, but a healthy cleaning out process. Belching, moving gas, and yawning will often increase the flow of saliva, and as the digestive system improves the saliva may become sweet and fragrant.

COLLECT THE ENERGY WHEN FINISHED

No matter where you end your practice, if you only concentrate on the navel, if you get as far as the Ming-men, or if you complete the route, at the conclusion of your practice you must always bring the energy back to your navel and collect it. Collecting the energy gathers up the excess chi in the body and stores it in the navel. It protects your body organs from accumulating too much energy.

To do this, concentrate on your navel as you place your right fist there. Then rotate your fist thirty-six times clockwise, allowing the circle to grow larger until it is no more than six inches in diameter (not higher than the heart nor lower than the pelvis). Then reverse the direction of rotation and rotate twenty-four times in a counterclockwise direction, gradually shrinking the circle until it returns to the navel. A woman reverses the order of rotation, first rotating counterclockwise thirty-six times and reversing the direction and shrinking the circle while rotating clockwise twenty-four times back to the navel. To determine direction imagine a clock at your navel.

DIAGRAM 24
A. Men finish by collecting the energy
in the navel and circling it 36 times clockwise
and 24 times counterclockwise.

B. Women finish by collecting the energy
in the navel and circling it
36 times counterclockwise
and 24 times clockwise.

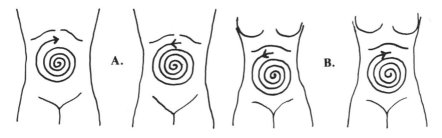

Eventually you will learn to direct the chi with your mind and will not need your fist to help you guide it.

Also, if you are short on time you can collect the energy three or nine times, reversing it the same number of times.

RUBBING THE FACE

During meditation, the hands will become very warm because of the Warm Current passing through them. Immediately after practice, rub your hands together briefly and then rub them briskly over your face for one or two minutes. This will serve, literally as a rejuvenating cosmetic substance. Rub your eyes gently and rotate them. Then rub your ears. Beat your teeth together lightly thirty-six times and finally rub your waist, legs, hands and soles of the feet. We will deal with this extensively in the Book of Tao Chi Massage.

DIAGRAM 25
Rejuvenate the skin by rubbing your face
after meditation with Chi flowing through the hands.

CHAPTER 7

OPEN THE ARM AND LEG ROUTES: THE LARGE HEAVENLY CYCLE

Once you have completed the microcosmic orbit, and feel competent circulating the energy, you are ready to direct the power to the arms and legs in addition to the main body trunk.

1. Begin with the basic orbit, concentrating on the navel until you feel warmth or energy, directing the chi down to the Hui-yin (perineum), up the spine to the Pai-hui (crown of head), and through the tongue and palate back to the navel. Stop at the navel to collect more energy, then direct the power once more to the Hui-yin (perineum).

2. From the Hui-yin divide the energy into two routes, directing the chi down the outer back portion of the left and right thigh to the 14th energy center, the back of the knee (Wei-Chung).

3. Next, move the energy down the outer calf to the 15th energy center, the Yin-chuan at the soles of the feet.

This is the first point of the kidney channel, and concentrating at this center will strengthen the kidney, lower blood pressure, and help relieve fatigue as more energy is brought to the feet.

Yung-chaun is often referred to as the "Bubbling Spring", or the point where the yin energy bubbles up from the earth and enters the soles of the feet. Many people who concentrate on the navel feel warmth in the feet instead, because the Yung-chuan is the origin of the energy that collects in the navel.

Concentrate at the soles until you feel energy there, then direct the chi to the 16th energy center which is located in the big toes. Both the liver and spleen (Ta-Tun and Yin Pai) meridians flow through the big toes and concentrating here will strengthen those organs. If you feel numbness or a pain like an ant bite, move the energy to the 17th energy center, the front of the knees (Heding).

4. To reach the 17th energy center, the chi travels up along the shin bone to the front of the knees. The stomach and spleen channels pass through this region, and opening this center will strengthen these organs as well as the knee, and prepare the passage for energy to go through at a later time. Be sure to draw the energy up from the earth through the soles of the feet to the knees.

5. When you sense warmth or tingling, shift your attention back to the Hui-yin (perineum), by directing the energy along the insides of the thighs.

6. Now send the energy to the Chang-chiang (coccyx), the Ming-men (opposite the navel), the Chi-chung (opposite the solar plexus), up to the mid-point of the scapulae.

7. Here the energy divides into the left and right arms and descends to the inside of the upper arms, down to the forearms, and passes along the middle of the palm, the Lao-kun. Concentrate here for a while and then feel the energy run along to the middle finger. Then go up the outside of the forearm along the outside of the middle of the upper arms, reaching the shoulder region. Here the energy rejoins on the spine between the shoulder blades.

8. Continuing on to the neck and up into the crown, allow the chi to descend to the tongue, where it finds its way back to the navel again, thereby completing the Microcosmic Orbit.

The Large Heavenly Orbit is part of the Fusion of the Five Elements. The second level of the Taoist Esoteric Yoga, Fusion of the Five elements, opens the other 6 psychic channels plus the Microcosmic (2 channels) which equals 8 channels.

DIAGRAM 26
When the Leg Route is completed,
Chi descends down to the soles of the feet
and up to the Hui-Yin.

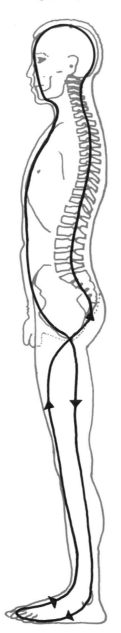

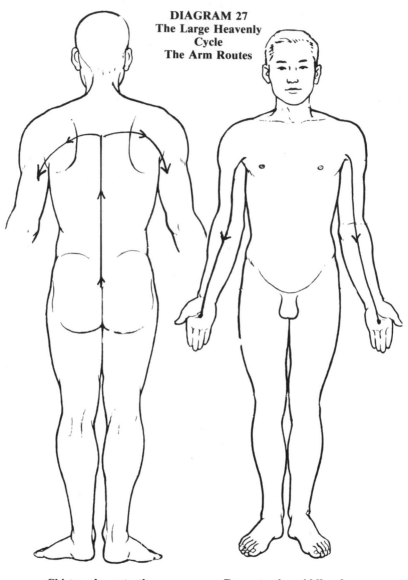

DIAGRAM 27
The Large Heavenly
Cycle
The Arm Routes

Chi travels up to the
mid-point of scapulae
and divides into the
arms.

Down to the middle of
the palm

DIAGRAM 28
The Large Heavenly Cycle
The Arm Routes

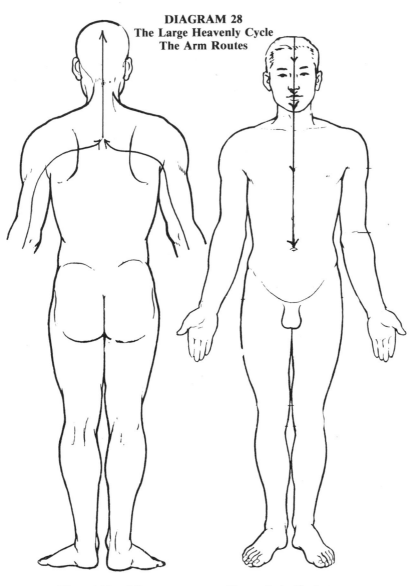

Up outside of the forearms, reaching the shoulder

Descends to the tongue and to the navel.

PART III:

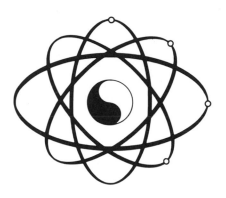

Practical Pointers

CHAPTER 8

SET A TRAINING SCHEDULE

A normal, healthy student should practice a half hour in the morning and a half hour in the evening. Someone who is sickly or weak should practice an hour in the morning, in the afternoon, and in the evening. Those who do not have back trouble, high blood pressure or gastric ulcers should do the "stretching the tendons exercise. This is done in nine sets of nine repetititions or three sets in the morning, afternoon and evening, making a total count of 81 for the day.

Do not worry if you miss a session. Just stay relaxed and if you can find a few odd minutes at home or in the office, try to meditate in those spare moments.

When first beginning it takes a little bit of time and discipline to achieve rapid progress. Remember that later on it will occur with no effort.

The exact amount of training and practice required to develop the Microcosmic Circulation varies from individual to individual. For best results one should practice at least twice a day at home, for ten to thirty minutes at a time, even if one has attained a higher level of accomplishment. Students with previous discipline in yoga or other meditation techniques are frequently able to open the microcosmic orbit immediately by redirecting their power of concentration away from the "third eye" (brow point) and into the warm current flow.

It is possible that some individuals might not succeed at all and never be able to grasp the essentials. Many report completion of the circulation within the first one hundred days of diligent practice. Most students report success within three months to a year. Improvement of illness may occur quite early in the practice. Many who worked hard on it, were reported to have achieved relief of their medical problems despite the seeming absence of a dramatic feeling of the "warm current" flow.

The Esoteric Taoist system of meditation ultimately leads to mastery of the "Third Eye" center, the crown of the head and those centers beyond. But it stresses the necessity of mastering all the lower energy centers first to insure a solid foundation for spiritual growth and self-healing.

There are spiritual "geniuses" on earth who can quickly transcend and stabilize themselves in higher energy centers. But most people cannot safely absorb this higher energy without first purifying the body and its lower energy centers. This may be a long and arduous process for some. The microcosmic orbit circulation is a safe and systematic approach to quickly achieve this transformation within the body. But only practice makes perfect, the greater your self-discipline the faster you will be rewarded with a marked increase in energy available to you.

REVIEW: THE MAJOR POINTS OF
THE MICROCOSMIC ORBIT

1. Sit easily and erectly on a chair with your right hand clasped over your left. Your chest should not be held up but be allowed to collapse slightly, while the head is tilted a bit forward. Count your breath, now, either from 1 to 10 or 10 to 1, doing this 10 times. This is done for its calming effect. When you have practiced in this way for some time you can dispense with counting. More advanced practitioners are immediately calmed upon assuming their seats.

2. Next on the agenda is abdominal breathing. This is done to stimulate the internal organs. In this method, exhale your breath by contracting the abdomen, compressing and massaging the organs therein and acting as an adjunct to the function of the dia-

phragm as it rises to compress the chest cavity. When you inhale, the diaphragm descends and again there is a compression and massage of the abdominal organs. This helps bring the Chi (or life force enegy) into the abdomen where it can be collected and utilized more effectively.

3. Breathe in this way for 36 cycles. After you feel calmed and concentrated and the energy is experienced in the abdomen you can practice progressive relaxation. This is accomplished by the method of "smiling" in the eyes and extending the feeling to the rest of the body, as has already been described. When you have completed this, down to "smiling" in your toes and fingers, use the index finger of your right hand to point at your navel. This is to be your point of concentration, unless you have high blood pressure.

In the latter case you are advised to concentrate, instead, on the soles of your feet. If you have heart burn or an extended chest, you should concentrate on the Ming-men, the point in back, opposite your navel. If you have low blood pressure, bring your index finger to the area between your eyebrows and bear down on it, maintaining the pressure for a few moments, so that when you've taken your finger away, the residual sensation helps in keeping your mind on the selected point.

4. If you practice using the navel area in the prescribed manner to develop Chi, it usually takes two weeks to a month before you feel anything. Once you do feel the energy there, you should shift your attention down to the sperm palace, which is near the pubic bone and represents the prostate gland. Young people who do this may be too sexually aroused, in which case they should instead focus on the coccyx or Ming-men. Women are to concentrate 3 inches down from the navel, which is where the ovaries are to be found. However, those who have menstrual problems are referred to the Ming-men or coccyx, instead of the navel. After that you can switch to concentrating on the Hui-yin (or perineum).

5. Some people may feel power very rapidly rise up the back when they place attention on the perineum and so they ought to concentrate, instead, on the coccyx. Before actually concentrating on either of these places, however, it helps to sit and rock back and forth on them. The coccyx has an opening called the hiatus. Rock-

ing on that and focusing your attention on it can sometimes lead to a very rapid channeling of chi or your back. When it does happen, concentrate on the navel.

6. After you have practiced for two months or so you can concentrate directly on the navel. That is, you don't have to count your breath or do the deep abdominal breathing — though you can do it, if you like. From the navel, the Chi should go to the ovary or sperm palace, the Hui-Yin, coccyx and up to the Ming-men on the back. Remain here until the power pushes up to the adrenal gland. ALWAYS REMEMBER TO FOLLOW THE ENERGY FLOW AND NOT FORCE IT.

7. The power ascends, thereafter, to the level of the shoulder blades and then the neck. Do not concentrate on the adrenals too long as this can cause insomnia. If you find this happening, concentrate on the coccyx. This will again send power up the back and into the small brain. When this is concentrated on you may feel your back get warm and you may find yourself unintentionally doing yoga-style breathing.

8. In time you may feel something in the top of your head in the pineal gland area. The energy, when encountered here, feels warm or numb and as though something were pressing from inside. From there, the Chi flows down to the mid-eyebrow region, making it feel very tight. Once you've reached this point, the Chi has completed the "Governor Route". Thereafter, the power must be directed downward, no matter what your level of development.

9. When you've reached the head, reverse it and direct it to the Ming-men, directing it from there to the inner sides of the thighs and ending in the soles. Concentrate there for a while and then bring your attention to your toes, knees, Hui-yin and then navel again. Stay there for a while and then go up one center to the solar plexus and concentrate there. Since you've opened the functional route, as soon as you concentrate on the solar plexus, you should feel energy there and in the area between the eyebrows as well. The energy that is developed at this time flows in both the Governor and Functional routes. Doing it this way is much safer and spares you side effects.

10. When you've developed more power, it will push up from the solar plexus into the heart chakra. This should be your next

point of concentration, then, but if you spend too much time here you will develop heart burn and find difficulty in breathing.

11. If you've concentrated for one or two weeks and the power has not yet risen to the throat energy center, you can either direct your attention to that center during your practice sessions or concentrate on your solar plexus and allow the energy to push its own way up to the throat center. When the power does get to the tip of your nose. This is a crucial point. Think the energy up to the tongue from the throat area and bring the energy in the brow area or nose down to the palate. When the energy descends along the nose, this causes some practitioners to sniffle (so that you can have some guide as to what might be happening).

Your tongue may seem to grow warm. When the proper place on the palate has been touched, you will feel as though you had a small electric shock in your tongue. When this happens, it marks the completion of the Microcosmic Orbit by the fusion of the Functional and Governor routes, known as the small heavenly cycle. This can later include your arms and legs, at which time you are said to have completed the full Microcosmic Orbit within the large Heavenly Cycle.

12. Everyone, regardless of age, must conclude their practice by directing the energy downward. Collect it in the navel and circulate it from 3 to 36 times in either direction. This is absolutely essential as a precaution against energy getting "stuck" in some other parts of the body.

CIRCULATE CHI POWER CONTINUOUSLY IN THE ORBIT

When you have completed the route point by point you are ready to continuously circulate the "chi" power in the Microcosmic Orbit. It is the steady flow of this warm energy current that offers the most powerful results in the self-healing process.

1. To do this, when you concentrate, begin at the navel. When you feel the power, bring it down to the Hui-yin, the coccyx. Then up into the spinal cord, stopping at the Ming-men and then going on to the pineal gland, on top of the head, where you concentrate for about ten minutes.

2. After you feel the power flowing into the forehead, at the mid-brow region concentrate on the pituitary gland, (Yin-Tang) for anogher ten minutes. After that, bring the power down to the navel. Concentrate here for a short while until you sense some energy and then bring it down to the Hui-Yin again.

3. Then start the Microcosmic Orbit small heavenly cycle around the trunk of your body, circulating it thirty six rounds, by bringing the power to the coccyx and letting it flow up the spinal cord, to the Chi!Chung or the mid-point of the adrenal glands.

4. Count from one to ten repeatedly for one half hour for its calming, purifying and cleansing effect. When you are more advanced all you need do is concentrate on the point. You no longer need to count. Then bring your attention up to your head and stop at the Niwan-Kung, the pineal gland where you can again count from 1-10 for resting, purifying and cleansing.

5. Thereafter, bring it down to the Hui-Yin again. This is one round of the Micro Orbit and it is to be done thirty-six times. If you can do this every day, it will greatly improve your health. When you're through, you must remember to collect the power mentally and circle the navel 3 to 36 times clockwise, and then 3 to 24 times in a counter clock-wise direction.

THE FINAL GOAL IS:
AUTOMATIC CIRCULATION OF CHI

Many have found that when they have completed the orbit and practiced for a while that concentration on the navel causes the energy to flow through the Microcosmic Orbit instantly. They feel the power in the head (the crown), and the mid-eyebrow area, instantly upon feeling the navel get warm. This is because the energy flows as a complete stream. The tongue might feel warm or numb, as though from an electrical shock. The flow can actually be felt to descend down to the navel and go into the legs. A feeling of numbness may be experienced in the arms and legs, when the big circuit of the Microcosmic Orbit of the large heavenly cycle has been completed.

Eventually the warm current will flow through your body automatically if you're creating a positive, permanent habit of circulating chi around the microcosmic orbit. Once your body/mind has internally absorbed the new pattern of chi flow, it will seek to maintain the dynamic equilibrium and circulate the chi automatically. Your weeks or months of self-discipline will begin bearing the fruit of a lifetime of delightful good health.

DIAGRAM 29
The Microcosmic Orbit

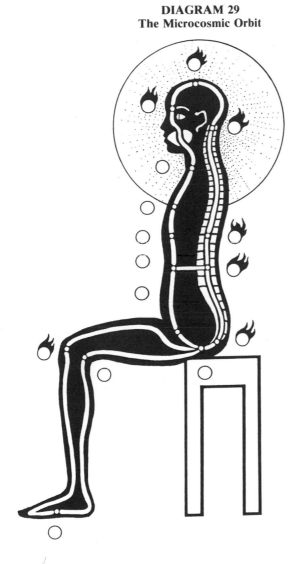

CHAPTER 9

THE SAFETY VALVES:
HOW TO PREVENT SIDE EFFECTS

You may find circulating chi to the navel point is quite comfortable, but when the power moves up to the head you may discover that you are easily irritated and sometimes have headaches. Concentrating on the heart chakra, you may develop congestion and pain in the chest and heart area. Be assured, however, that though you may initially suffer some untoward effects, your continued practice will set you free of all such symptoms. However, it must be stressed that you keep your instructor alerted to whatever you might experience so that he will be able to help you. Make sure to finish each session by returning the energy to the navel and circling it 3 to 36 times clockwise and 3 to 24 times counter clockwise for a man, and the reverse for a woman.

The following centers can act as safety valves, thus helping to avoid side effects: 1) the navel can store energy, 2) the Ming-men on the back of the spine helps guide the energy downward, 3) the Wei-Chung (the back of the knee) can store up energy, 4) the Yung-Chuan in the feet acts as a grounding wire. The Hung-Chaun energy center can also be used as a safety valve to draw off energy that builds in the head. When too much energy surges up to the heart and seems to have no place to go, you can redirect it downward to the feet and then up to the navel.

THE CLEANSING PROCESS:
BELCHING AND DIARRHEA

People who, develop belching and diarrhea during practice might think that it is due to something that they have eaten. This is not the case, however. When the power starts to flow, it acts as a cleansing and filtering agent for the body and the organs. The diarrhea that ensues is not the usual kind. After it is over you will feel very energetic and internally light and clean. You may feel a little weaker but you will feel much better than you can recall. Your stool may be very dark and sticky. This is classically explained as being due to the poisons that had accumulated in your esophagus, stomach, intestines and other organs over the years that are being cleaned out.

When this cleansing is completed, the diarrhea ceases and you reach another stage where you feel much calmer and cleaner. After this cleansing, you are advised to watch what you eat, curbing your intake of oily and spicy foods, fermented foods and meat. Essentially, you should eat less at a time and eat food that is fresh and of good quality. As you progress in your practice you will develop an intuitive awareness os what food is best for you at the time. An organ awareness will have been awakened, which will enable the needs of the body to be satisfied.

SEXUAL LIFE DURING PRACTICE

When one has just begun to train, sexual intercourse should be curbed considerably, if not altogether. Abstention will enable you to have the necessary energy to complete the routes. Opening the microcosmic orbit will eventually improve your sexual relations as you gain mastery over your body's energy system. Sex is a natural human act and if you can properly control and use it, you will enjoy it all the more. You will find more details on this in the book on SEMINAL KUNG FU, which demonstrates clearly how to have a more nourishing sex life.

Those who are weak and sick should abstain from sex for two to six months or until some degree of vitality has been regained.

APPETITE AND STOMACH AILMENTS

The most important thing to us is the stomach (the element of earth). Concentrating on the navel you may feel the area expand, as though with air. This sensation often extends up to the stomach, at which time you may be assailed by fits of belching and yawning . . . especially if you have some stomach disorder.

Raisng your tongue to your palate will increase the flow of saliva. When you have totally cleansed your stomach and intestines, the saliva will become much more sweet and fragrant.

THROAT CENTER: COUGHING

When you concentrate on the mid-point between your nipples, the power pushes up to the throat chakra. Many practitioners develop a cough when the power gets stuck, as it were, in pushing up from the chest and into the throat chakra. Some may even cough up dark sticky mucous at this time. Cleansing this point can help the power flow considerably. By the time it pushes up from the throat to the tongue you will feel calm and less worried. This does not mean that you will never have any worries or anxiety but it docs indicate that you will feel more calm and will be able to sit and meditate more easily.

Some Taoist books may seem to exaggerate the importance of the chakras as power centers but what we are talking about here is based on the actual experiences of many hundreds of students.

CLEANSING OF THE ESOPHAGUS,
STOMACH AND INTESTINES

The cleansing of the esophagus, the stomach and the intestines is very important, because food passes down this way and there are many places where it can lodge, causing some blockage. THE SIX HEALING SOUNDS describes how during that phase of training, there is belching as well as the passing of gas and yawning, marking another very important aspect of the cleansing process. It is advised that you drink one or two glasses of clear settled water in the morning one hour before breakfast to clean out your digestive system. After drinking the water it will also help to rub your stomach with both palms 9 times in both a clockwise and counter clockwise direction.

ILLUSIONS AND MENTAL ILLNESS

Those who tend to have illusions or mental illness must make sure that they direct the power back to the navel at the end of each practice session. This will help to prevent such afflictions and many other side effects. In fact, everyone should end his practice in this way on the off chance that some stress or weakness has been incurred somewhere that he may not know about. When practitioners who are in a weakened condition have more power made available to them, they may experience such effects as ringing of the ears, muffled hearing, or smarting eyes.

Once the power is activated, you will find that if you have ever had a toothache you may again experience it and if you have a latent virus or cold in your system it may be activated. Various other pains out of the past may suddenly assail you. It may seem as though the "power" is the cause of your trouble and it is, in a way, and you would be correct in thinking so.

Your problems and illnesses have remained hidden in your body, unknown to you. There are various ways to understand this. Perhaps it might make more sense to say that most of our ills stem from the mind. The mind is a storehouse of everything we have been exposed to and when we use it, opened and cleaned, the sickness will be overcome.

Initially, as you are suddenly confronted anew with painful memories relived as though they were real, you feel that your practice has caused this and it has. As you continue to practice, however, and as these mind contents are emptied and replaced by a harmoniously functioning system, you come to realize the wisdom of just how you personally have harbored and been affected by these "memory-illnesses".

That is not to say that the illness you experience was just in your imagination. The mind is complex and, in fact, are inseparable from the body. Perhaps, "body" is just another way to describe a complex set of processes that might, with another view, be called "mind" comes closer to it. Again, as the various energy routes are cleared of obstructions, it is conceivable that some of those obstructions might have been due to past illnesses or injuries. Then, as resistance to the flow of energy is met along a route, the memory that is associated with it is evoked.

WHEN TO SEE A DOCTOR

If you have definite physical problems you should follow your doctor's advice as well. You are not to think of this method as some sort of magical cure-all, and should seek to obtain whatever you need to improve your health, with whatever resources may be available. Problems most often arise in practice with those who are ill or in a weakened physical condition. If they want to progress rapidly, they would be well-advised to use a physician. A number of practitioners have had misgivings for thinking that they could depend solely upon their esoteric practice and never see a doctor again and have ended up with sad stories to tell. To help solve your health problems you should use what modern medicine offers and the Taoist practices you have learned, as well as anything else that you might have found to be effective, being careful to be open to the best choice for you.

PROPER PRACTICE WILL PREVENT SIDE EFFECTS

In awakening the life force energy of Taoist Esoteric practice each person is required in the first stage to open the Microcosmic Orbit. The Governor Channel corresponds to the route that is followed by awakened sperm energy rising from the coccyx to the crown of the head. The Tao System differs from the Indian in that a return route is provided for: from the palate to the tongue to the throat, to the navel and back to the coccyx to begin a new circuit. In this way, power is evenly distributed throughout the seven glands. There is far less pain in the head than one would have in Kundalini practice because a safety valve is afforded as a provision for distributing the pressure.

The seven glands act like a series of containers, within each of which the same level of fluid must be maintained. When this is done, all of the seven will function properly with none of them being stimulated more than it should be. This is exquisitely accomplished in the completion of the Microcosmic Orbit. With only one direction of flow through the containers, the lower or the upper one can be over expanded, which can result in malfunction and damage. With a return set of connections running to each container, however, the overflow can be taken up by the circuit and the other glands that it is connected to, resulting in reduced stress and a return to balance.

At higher levels of Taoist Chi circulation more routes are opened allowing more energy to flow but also creeating additional "safety valves". After the Microcosmic Orbit is completed an additional 30 routes in the whole body must be opened. When they have all been opened, the life force energy chi can freely flow through the organism, eliminating the side effects which might otherwise be caused by the over-stimulation of one gland or another. For example, if the adrenals are overstimulated you cannot sleep, because your pulse rate is alarmingly increased and you feel anxious and alert. If the power flows into the heart energy center and there is no means for it to flow out, the heart rate goes up drastically. The pericardium is supposed to function as a cooling system but is unable to do so under such circumstances. Something akin to this can also occur if the energy is not properly guided down along the front portion of the Microcosmic Orbit.

Finally, prevention is the safest approach to avoid ill side effects. As mentioned elsewhere, the singlemost important safeguard is to end your chi circulation practice at the navel point where it is circled in both directions from 3 to 36 times. In the beginning you should try to circle it the full 36 times; eventually you will discover the energy spins more quickly and this "closing off" will take only seconds.

CHAPTER 10

COMMONLY ASKED QUESTIONS & ANSWERS ON THE MICROCOSMIC

1. WHAT IS CHI, OR ELECTRO-MAGNETIC LIFE FORCE?

Chi, otherwise called the Warm Current, Kundalini Power or electro-magnetic life force, is very difficult to describe because this energy, or life force, cannot be seen. However, we can feel the life force in the body. In the early days of Tao, chi was expressed as nothing in the top portion of the Chinese pictogram and as fire in the lower part, so that no fire might be conceived of as defining Chi. More contemporary Taoist sources classify many kinds of Chi. There is pre-nature Chi, the kind you breathe, as well as the Chi that is transmuted in our bodies and the kind that has been awakened from sperm or ovary called Ching-chi.

Ching-Chi, the main energy source of our practice, is ultimately transformed into spiritual energy. We all have Chi from the time we are conceived. The taoist teaches us that life force or Chi begins as the energy you derive from the food you eat and the air you breathe. In Taoist practice, you draw on many different sources of energy, which reside in different energy centers in the body, such as the heart, adrenals, prostate, pineal and the pituitary. There is yet another kind of energy that we absorb from the solar system, mix and transform in our body, which produces still another kind of Chi in a process called ALCHEMY.

Taoism stresses practice and theory; philosophy and discussion are discouraged as futile. By a simple method of relaxation and concentratiing on your navel, you can experience for yourself what the flow of Chi is.

Several of my students had spent as many as five to twenty years trying to develop Chi and complete the Microcosmic Orbit, but to no avail. After a short time with me they completed their objectives in one to four months. They all found this method easy and natural. Spending just thirty to sixty minutes a day, many who developed power quickly thought that they were dreaming or that it was an act of imagination. Yet, when they practiced they felt warm and soon reported how much healthier they seemed to be getting.

2. DO YOU HAVE TO SIT IN A CHAIR?

We recommend sitting in a chair. This is the most comfortable position for most and is especially good for those people who have back and leg problems. It also allows chi to flow freely through the legs. Many people believe that if you assume the lotus position you will feel more rooted and will gradually limber, or already have very open energy routes in your legs, sitting in the lotus or quarter lotus can only interfere with energy flow and hamper your progress.

If we compare the head to root of a tree, through which we can absorb power from the heavens then we can compare the legs to the branches and leaves and so they are also very important in practice. When you attain a higher level of practice, you will find that the soles of your feet absorb Yin power from the Earth. Sitting in a chair facilitates directing the power down to the feet. When Chi is circulated in just the upper part of the body and not directed down to the feet, it is like having the leaves whither and fall off the tree. No matter how well you practice in the upper body, if the power has not flowed down to the legs, there is a very significant lack of energy and you simply cannot function properly. When Chi circulates in your legs you will feel lighter, will walk more erectly and will be able to walk longer distances without fatigue.

Using a chair is important for another reason, too. A man must let his testes hang freely so as to be able to properly absorb energy. As your practice progresses, you have to open six special routes and the flow has to run down to your feet. Sitting cross-legged makes it very difficult to direct the power, although some people claim that when you have been successful in collecting energy you can direct the power in any position.

I have known many monks who had leg problems, which might or might not have been caused by sitting cross-legged for too long. If you can direct power to your legs, there will be fewer problems, but since cross-legged sitting calls for more effort, it is not a wise practice nor an efficient one. Since at one stage of your development, you absorb energy from the earth through the soles of your feet, which necessitates having your feet flat on the ground, the position of choice, then, is sitting in a chair.

3. DURING PRACTICE, WHAT SHOULD MEN DO WHEN THEY GET AN ERECTION AND WHAT SHOULD WOMEN DO WHEN THE VAGINA SWELLS?

When this happens in men, the testes may feel as though they were vibrating, there might be a slight discharge of semen along with a sensation of pressure in the prostate gland, and the Hui-Yin may also seem to vibrate, whereas women may feel their vagina and nipples distending.

When you are able to practice and collect power, it will naturally flow down to your reproductive organs and stimulate sexual anxiety. To overcome this, shift your concentration back to the Ming-men and then bring it up to your head to the mid-point between your eyebrows. In the book on Seminal Kung Fu, we demonstrated very clearly (in the large drawing of the sexual force rising up to the crown) how one can make an erection subside. I have many male students who, after practicing, experience erection and have to find relief in sexual intercourse. Some of those students stopped practicing because their sexual urge was too overpowering. However, if you can control or stop your sexual activity for a while, or get your spouse to understand or practice together with you, you will achieve success in this practice much more quickly.

4. WILL CIRCULATING THE MICROCOSMIC HELP MY SEXUAL PROBLEMS?

For those who are impotent, ejaculate too quickly or who have emmissions; when they concentrate a while, they may feel pain or expansion in the back. This may cause an erection and may result in night emissions or a loss of sperm while urinating.

When you concentrate you are in fact preserving and storing life force, which is then first drawn to the reproductive organs and it is this which increases your sex urge. If you can retain these life forces, however, your overall health will be greatly benefitted. It is safe to say that those who are weaker have been driven by lust. Those who are impotent should stop all sexual activity for from 3 to 6 months, consult a doctor and practice until they find themselves getting stronger. To practice and acquire some energy and then have an erection and go right back to sexual activity is simply to have lost what you have worked so hard to gain in your practice. When you have collected energy and fully completed the route, your body will become stronger and only then will you be able to enjoy your sexual life.

5. IS TAOIST PRACTICE SUITABLE FOR EVERYONE?

Generally speaking, it should be good for everyone. But those who have physical problems or who suffer from mental or emotional problems, should be careful in their practice. In the Taoist system, we start by training the body and then the soul and finally venture into spiritual development. Taoism describes the body as a boat or ship. A perfect ship is a perfect body and a good engine is a good soul. The spirit is described as a diamond which we want to send to its destination. But if you do not have a good ship and a good engine you cannot deliver the diamond to its goal. Some people do not pay attention to the body and seek just to protect the diamond and the diamond sinks into the sea before they can reach their goal.

In the Taoist System and in others as well, one begins by strengthening the body. Thus, it is very unlikely that you will allow a young, childish spirit to wander in dangerous and unknown lands.

When you open the thirty-two routes, the soul and spirit have room to travel within the body. As you progress you have to learn how to train the soul, how to mingle the body with the soul. Join and train this combination with the spirit, so that it, too, is included in a new mix and gradually the dangers of the practice are reduced.

6. CAN WOMEN PRACTICE DURNG MENSTRUATION?

Women who have trouble with menstruation should discontinue practice for the duration. Those who have irregular bleeding should not concentrate on the Kuan-yuan, which is three inches down from the navel, as this is the energy center of the ovary. They should concentrate, instead, on the point between the eyebrows and on the Door of Life (Ming-men).

7. SHOULD I CONCENTRATE ON THE "THIRD EYE" BETWEEN THE EYEBROWS?

One must be careful when concentrating on this point. The power tends to flow upward and if it is obstructed, possibly because the palate is too thick, and it is harder for the Chi to penetrate it then to rise up and push open the Pai-hui in the crown of the head. This forces it to flow out of the body for some time, and may cause pressure to build in the head. Therefore, young people, strong virile types, those with high blood pressure and those with mental problems should not concentrate on this point.

8. WHY DO SOME PRACTITIONERS DEVELOP PAINS IN THE BACK OR SHOULDERS DURING PRACTICE?

I have many students who experience pain or tightness and pressure in the back after concentrating for some time. This depends upon one's body condition. Most young people and healthy adults who exercise regularly will often find that when they sit and the power goes into the back, pushing up through the spinal column, needle-like sensations develop because that route had been obstructed for so long. If you simply relax and concentrate, let us say, on the Ming-men and do not pay attention to how it is going, the power will push up by itself.

If you try to assist in this process by pushing or in any way forcing, you will begin to feel nervous and uncomfortable and the power will get stuck in the back, producing pain. When the power reaches the Ja-chi, just concentrate there. Thereafter, allow the power to continue ascending from the upper back to the neck and then to the Yu-chen, No. 7, or the small brain, which includes the cerebrum and the cerebellum.

Try to concentrate on this energy center and when the power finally pushes up to the Bei-huei, you will feel free and very comfortable and the pain, tightness and discomfort in your back will disappear. Sometimes, the power may seem to push outward from the spinal column, not into it, at which time there will be no such tightness and discomfort.

BACK PAIN FOR OLDER AND WEAKER PEOPLE

When sick or elderly people who are burdened by weak lungs, stomach, liver, heart or other internal ailments, concentrate for some time, they may have much pain in the back and shoulders. There might even be sensations of heat and cold in the affected areas. One must keep in mind that concentration activates a natural process of healing. Those who have illneses that are hidden ailments will come out of hiding, so that they are once again afflicted as they had been in the past.

9. CAN PEOPLE THAT HAVE HAD SURGERY PRACTICE?

Taoist training will help those who have had major or minor surgery to recover faster. After they practice for a while they may, however, feel pain at the site of the incision. This effect is actually a good sign, which indicates that the power is healing the cut from the inside. When the pain disappears, it means that the wound has been thoroughly healed. You might even have had an operation a long time ago and no longer have any pain, but once the power begins to flow, it will alert you exactly to where the pain was.

10. WHY DO SOME PEOPLE EXPERIENCE RINGING IN THE EARS DURING PRACTICE?

This will happen when the power ascends into the brain and it is sometimes the result of energy vibrating in the ear (the bony inner ear). Practitioners respond differently to it. Some like it and think that it means that they are making progress, while others are convinced that something has gone wrong and are frightened. If they can calm down and practice swallowing saliva, it will help to keep the eustachean tube open which equalizes pressure on the ear drums and can facilitate hearing.

They should then try to relax the head and back and bring their attention to the Ming-men, allowing the power to flow down to it from the head. Furthermore, after they have felt some relief, they can finish by bringing their attention to the navel for a while before rotating around it mentally or by using one hand first clockwise 36 times and then counter-clockwise 24 times (the direction is opposite for women). It might also help to feel all the power being gathered to this point as one is doing this. Bear in mind that the energy goes where the mind directs it.

11. WHAT SHOULD ONE DO WHEN, AFTER PRACTICING FOR SOME TIME, ONE LOSES ONE'S APPETITE?

After concentrating on the navel and then the Ming-men in the back, some people report having their appetite improve. They then eat well and find their bowel function improved. After the power travels up to the back of the head and then goes to the Pai-hui, they might report having difficulty in breathing, losing their appetite and developing trouble with their bowel movement. This happens when the power has been blocked and has not been properly or sufficiently directed back to the navel. Be patient and circle it down, as has just been described above, drink more water and eat more fruit and all of the symptoms will fade away. Remember, then, that if you direct the power back down to the navel at the end of each practice period, this problem will not occur.

12. WHY IS IT THAT, AFTER PRACTICING FOR A WHILE, SOME PEOPLE JERK ABOUT SPASMODICALLY, ASSUME YOGA POSITIONS OR ELICIT VARIOUS SOUNDS?

Shaking is not an unusual effect and is, in fact, beneficial, serving as an internal exercise. Concentrating on just one thought has been known to stop it and if it becomes really violent you can end it simply by ordering it to stop. However, I encourage everyone to shake for the benefits they can derive from it. To do this, they can either pretend that they are shaking or concentrate on the navel, exhaling as though into the stomach and through the back. If they continue to exhale until they no longer can, they will begin to shake. To stop this shaking, just order it to stop and breathe normally.

DIAGRAM 30
Bursts of Chi energy may cause shaking of the body.

Shaking and jerking about during practice is caused by nervousness or psychological problems hidden within the mind. Some practitioners who are very suggestable may have read about what happens and it happens to them. Others seem to shake in a logical way, which means that if they move the left hand in a circle thirty six times, then they will move the right hand thirty-six times too. There are those who are very frightened when this happens.

As the Chi, or the energy of the heart, liver, spleen, lungs, kidneys, fills the organs, there are specific reactions expressed as various "shakings".

1. The heart controls the veins and arteries. The Chi of the heart causes the body to jump up and down like a monkey at play. (This shows that the Heart Meridian is full of Chi).

2. The liver controls the tendons. When it fills with Chi, the big toes and legs may cramp as the Chi swims joyfully in the ocen of divine ecstasy, like a fish.

3. The spleen controls the muscles and when they fill with Chi, they jump like a bird hopping from one branch to another. The place where it rests feels like fire. This is because the vital Chi of the spleen is moving around.

4. The lungs control the skin. When they fill with Chi you will feel prickly itching and heat all over the body, as though ants were crawling over you, especially on your face. This is because the vital Chi of the lung is moving around.

5. The kidneys control the bones. When they fill with Chi you will hear the sound of the moving bone. Moving up the spine like a snake, it sometimes causes sexual arousal.

If you shake too much, the power will scatter and not run in the Microcosmic Orbit. Shaking sends the power into the tendons, muscles, limbs and organs, and is good for those who want to strengthen those parts. I recommend that students sit for half an hour, shake for five or ten minutes and then stop and concentrate on the power flow. The shaking can be both intentional and unintentional. Doing this often limbers one up, thereby aiding concentration and clearing Chi channels.

When one begins practice and has not yet completed the Microcosmic Orbit, however, I usually advise that he not allow shaking to occur. When you let the power flow by itself, all sorts of seemingly automatic things happen if you just go with whatever seems to be happening. This is a very good exercise for releasing tension and stress.

13. HOW DOES CHI AFFECT THE SICK BODY?

When the energy reaches a diseased organ it circles the area. For example, if you have a kidney condition, you should be able to feel the energy moving for a set number of times to the left and the right around the two kidneys. If you have stomach or intestinal problems, the energy will move in the direction of the stomach and your body will shake. Those who have a heart problem will find that the energy lodges around the heart. When people who have a heart or liver problem engage in this practice and suddenly have difficulty in breathing and a feeling of distress and congestion in the chest, they may think that the system itself is not good and want to stop practicing.

I have had a few students who have had just this problem arise. They went to see doctors who were not familiar with Chi-kung or the Microcosmic Circulation and who assumed the trouble came from practicing "meditation". In fact, the energy had been opening blockages, which had been there for some time. Long before they began practicing, they had sometimes felt their heart beat very quickly and had become short of breath but had never attached any importance to it.

It was only because they had ventured into somethiing new and different when they started to practice that they grew alarmed because the symptoms remained too long. It may help to know that it is the nature of this practice to have such things happen until health is restored. If they break off with their practice they simply continue to suffer, growing steadily worse. If the power is able to get through the blockage in the chest, there may be vomiting or diarrhea but after that is done with, a level of well-being will be achieved never previously known.

14. HOW DO YOU REMEDY BLOCKAGE IN THE CHEST?

In order to avoid the unpleasant side-effects that occur when the power is blocked in the chest, redirect it down to Ming-men and concentrate there, instead. If that doesn't seem to help, shift your attention to another power center, perhaps the Hsuan-Chi, and concentrate there for a while until you feel the power move up.

I have had a number of students who, for one reason or another, did not respond well in their practice and so I advised that they concentrate on their navel. After a period of weeks or months, I'd received various distress calls from them as the power developed sufficiently to make itself known. One young lady kept saying that nothing was happening, until, after about three months, she called in great distress to report that she was having pain in her chest and difficulty in breathing. I knew immediately what had happened. She had continued to concentrate on her navel, even though I had advised her to switch to her Ming-men in her lower back. The pain and symptoms she now had were simply due to the energy having risen up the front meridian into her chest. Had she been concentrating on her Ming-men, the channel that would have been available there would have been in her back and she wouldn't have had the trouble she described.

15. WHAT IS THE PROPER TIME TO PRACTICE AND MUST YOU DO IT REGULARLY?

The Taoists divide the time for practice into four periods. At six o'clock in the morning, less Yin, more Yang; at 12:00 noon, strong Yang, at six o'clock in the evening, less Yang, more Yin; and at midnight, strong Yin. The length of time should be fifteen to thirty minutes at the beginning. As you make progress you can then extend it to one hour. Most importantly, find your own time and practice regularly every day. It is of no use, if you practice one day for three hours and then stop for two or three months. Ideally, begin your practice regularly, for fifteen to twenty minutes each day and expand as you make progress.

16. DO PEOPLE WHO PRACTICE THIS METHOD HAVE TO WATCH THEIR DIET?

You should eat whatever your body tells you to eat. It is not necessary to be strictly vegetarian. If you can become vegetarian, however, and your body feels good with it, then that is the best thing for you. If you eat too much meat, garlic or onions, it will arouse you sexually, which will interfere with your practice. I would advise you to abstain or at least to greatly curb your sexual activity until you have gathered sufficient power and have opened enough Chi routes. Until that time, remember that the most important thing for you to do is to retain your sperm and ovary energy because it is a great source of energy.

If you lose much sperm or seminal fluid, your energy reserve will be very low and it is hard to produce Chi otherwise. As soon as you begin to conserve energy through this practice, you will have more erections at night or during practice.

It is very important to try to curb them. To do this, try to breathe and draw in energy from the Hui-Yin and from the tip of the penis, directing it up through the back to your head.

17. I HAVE SOME FRIENDS WHO, AFTER LEARNING THESE METHODS, DO NOT SEEM INTERESTED IN SOCIAL ACTIVITY. WILL YOU COMMENT ON THIS?

This is not the point of practice, although there are some people who, after having begun training, would rather live away from people. The main purpose is to make yourself stronger and happier and not to run away from things. The Taoist approach is concerned with harmony and so we suggest that people marry and lead a happy family life, so that they can practice more effectively and achieve their goals more quickly. There is no need to run away from the world or from your family. If you can't control your heart in the city, you willnever control yourself in the jungle either. Remember, if you can practice well at home, you can practice anywhere.

18. CAN RELAXATION AND CONCENTRATION CUT DOWN ON THE NUMBER OF HOURS YOU SLEEP?

Sleep is most important. Through sleep you are able to recover energy, allowing the body to refuel and repair itself. So it would be wrong, especially at the start, to substitute meditation for sleep.

In the beginning, practice is practice and sleep is sleep. Some people think that sitting in meditation is just the same as sleep. It is true that meditation will calm down your nervous system and brain but your body still needs the rest and sleep is the best way of providing it. If you sleep less and then tend to fall asleep during practice, that is not good at all. Not being able to concentrate during practice you will simply defeat your own purpose.

Try to have regular hours of sleep. The average adult needs about eight hours. It is said, traditionally, that when Chi fills all of your organs and you fulfill the rebirth process, your body will need less sleep. Yet, we must recognize that living in these times, subjected as we are to different kinds of stress, new rules must apply.

19. HOW DOES PRACTICING THE MICROCOSMIC AFFECT YOUR EMOTIONS? SHOULD YOU PRACTICE WHEN ANGRY, SAD, OR DISAPPOINTED?

All these feelings will affect your practice. Because we live in a stressful world, no one is able to live a really happy or satisfactory life. Try to be content and satisfied with what you have. When you become discouraged, do some exercise, take a long walk, or find some other way to calm down and then have a good sleep and in time you will feel better. There are many methods that are helpful. You can chant or count your breaths or repeat mantras.

All of these divert your attention from your trouble and set you at ease. But remember always to smile and relax. There are added benefits to this practice. You will find that you will become calmer and more stable and may no longer lose your temper as readily. So it is safe to say that as you become healthier you will be less angry. This has happened to many of my students. No matter how much psychology you have studied or theories you have understood or lectures you have attended about how to control your anger and your mind, if you do not actually practice, you will make no progress.

Many of my students have told me that they have had philosophy up to their necks but that it does not really help them. What we are trying to tell you is that you will find out you have completed the route and have harmonized the Yin and Yang in your body, you will feel happier, less angry and will be able to take more sttress. You will see the world as beautiful and see all people as saints. By contrast, if you are sick and frightened as a mouse, when you see people, even good, kind people who want to help you, you will believe that they want to harm you.

Your main aim now should be to make your body, your nervous system, soul, spirit, your whole being — healthy, by means of this training. Try to remind yourself to smile and do one good thing each day. That is all you need. You do not have to depend on a higher master to guide your spirit; your spirit is yours. No one else can guide your spirit. If your spirit has to depend on others for guidance, then you are in trouble.

20. DOES RHYTHMIC BREATHING OR CHANTING HELP TO CIRCULATE THE MICROCOSMIC ORBIT?

Generally, it does not. I may advise some students to do it in the very beginning to help them calm down, but urge them to get along without it as soon as possible. All that is called for is that you concentrate on the energy center or centers that you are working on. If you pay attention to your breathing, the power or the warm current will not concentrate itself at the center but will scatter.

I have many students who had been practicing for many years (some for as much as twenty or thirty years) who told me that they had never felt any unusual energy in all their years of practice. When they came to me I told them to just concentrate on the points and not to pay attention to breathing. Many of them, in their first session, often after just a few minutes of concentration, experienced bliss and power, and found themselves deep in concentration. All of these students were well prepared and had a lot of energy in reserve, but didn't know how to turn it on and have it flow in the proper channels.

There are countless methods of breathing and they all make it very hard to feel the "warm currents". If you can concentrate on the point assigned to you and do not pay attention to the breath. If you can put everything out of your mind and just concentrate on that point, the power will flow freely. When you concentrate, you casually watch the point. There is no straining, no great act of will power, but just passive watching. In this situation of just watching you will feel very calm. So don't pay any attention to the breathing, just watch the energy center.

21. DOES MASTER CHIA PASS ENERGY TO HIS STUDENTS TO HELP OPEN THE ROUTES?

When someone first comes to me, I may give them energy. Upon being touched some people experience the warm current in a few minutes. The body may feel as though affected by an electric shock and start to vibrate and go into deep concentration. By merely describing the route of the energy flow to them and without my touching them, they go into deep concentration, feel energy running through their body and have an irregular and sometimes rapid and shallow breathing pattern. Someone came to me just one time and completed the route, experiencing great inner beauty, peace, and a deep knowledge of his innermost self. That happens, too.

22. ARE THERE ANY SIDE EFFECTS WITH YOUR METHOD?

In China, Taoists have been studying, experiencing, passing all of their lifetime experiences down to us for 8,000 years. We know the route and so it is very easy to guide one along. The nature of the warm current or Chi is that it tends to flow up to the head, which is the most important part of the nervous system. If it gets stuck there, and you don't know how to bring it down, it can damage the brain. By gradually exposing yourself to increasingly larger amounts of energy, however, it is possible to adjust to it. The price for not allowing enough time to adjust and of affording enough safeguards is an overload, which can result in pain, fear, outright injury and insanity. There are those who succeed quickly by pushing power into the head without side effects, but they are the exceptions.

The Microcosmic is a safe system because once the two main channels are open, the energy will circulate automatically in a loop. Energy flowing in a circle will never build up enough energy at any single point to cause serious discomfort or pain. But if you try to force the energy to flow in one direction only, such as to the higher centers in the head, it may burst like a water hose with a kink in it. The water pressure has no where to go but explode.

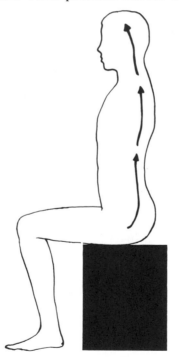

Additional safety routes are available in this Taoist practice. If too much energy gets stuck in the head, just reverse the flow and send the energy down the back to the feet and then up the front to the tongue/palate. Putting the tongue up to the palate completes the circuit, joining the energy of the Governor and Functional channel. It is like building a tunnel through a mountain; it will shorten the time if you dig from both ends and meet at the middle. This is what we are doing when we join the two routes into a single loop.

23. WHY DO I FEEL TIRED AFTER MEDITATING?

The warm current concentration is an exercise of the mind, which directs the current and burns large quantities of energy in the course of purifying the nervous systems of the organism. During the early stages of practice you will be doing a great deal of repair work on your body. After concentrating you may feel tired or experience some soreness in your back. The Taoist rebirth process explains itself. It is a means whereby the sick and damaged body recreates the life process to that of a baby. To accomplish this, one needs a lot of material and energy. Those who are strong and healthy will find that after practice they feel refreshed. Those who are ill or unhealthy, or who think they are healthy but in fact are not, will feel sleepy or tired in the beginning when such energy is expended in a virtual repair and rebuilding process. One gradually changes into a stronger, more vigorous and yet peaceful person. Remember that this method calls for gradual change and a restructuring of the entire individual. As toxins are flushed out and tissues are replaced, you may find that eating a handful of grapes or other sweet, juicy fruit will help disperse fatigue. The longer you practice the better you will feel. After the period of tissue repair is completed, you will feel strengthened by your practice sessions.

24. WHAT IS THE BENEFIT OF COMPLETING THE MICROCOSMIC ORBIT?

The Microcosmic is the basic tool of the Taoist system. By circulating chi in this simple orbit you are generating energy to be stored in the navel. The body knows which organs are in need of extra energy. When circulating the warm current the organs, glands, and blood automatically receive this energy.

PART IV:

Healing Applications of
Tao Energy

The Microcosmic helps the body resist sickness by keeping the energy in harmony. The inner smile is the model of loving yourself with pure, unconditional love. By practicing the inner smile and circulating chi in the Microcosmic Orbit we come to understand our body on a deeper level and learn to create love, respect and self-esteem within ourselves. Our body is potentially a perfect machine to serve our mind and spirit. But we can have a perfect machine only if each part functions harmoniously with the others.

The Microcosmic enables you to put an 8,000 year old discovery by Chinese Masters into use in your daily life. Its applications are endless. Continued practice can bring greater calmness, clarity, and energy to every aspect of your current life. By circulating chi in the orbit, you also open the door to discovering priceless higher knowledge of the tao, he harmonious way of nature.

CHAPTER 11

MEDICAL SCIENCE LOOKS
AT THE MICROCOSMIC

A MEDICAL OPINION ON THE
BENEFIT OF TAOIST CHI CIRCULATION
BY C.Y. HSU, M.D.

For over two thousand years the theory of Chi has been the basis of classical Chinese medical practice. Chi is said to flow through a system of channels in the body; when the flow of Chi is disturbed for whatever reason, illness results. Medical treatment aims to re-establish the normal flow of Chi and thus restore one's health.

Unlike the circulation of blood, the flow of Chi is difficult to document objectively. For several decades many scientists throughout the world attempted to demonstrate the existence of such a system of Chi-channels with no success.

When I heard about Master Chia's method of Chi development I was fascinated and decided to try it. After four months practice, I began to sense a consistent feeling of warmth developing inside my abdomen. Soon after, under Master Chia's guidance, I was able to direct the flow of this energy through the major channels of my body at will. Not only did this curious form of energy travel along pathways as described in classical Chinese medical literature but the energy would dwell at sites corresponding precisely to the major classical acupuncture points.

If there is a system of energy flowing through the body, then it is logical to assume that the maintenance of such a flow in a normal and efficient state is important. In Master Chia's method of developing Chi-flow, there is a tremendous possibility for development of one's physical and mental well being.

C.Y. Hsu, M.D.
Clinical Assistant Professor of
Anesthesiology
Physician-in-charge of Acupuncture and
Nerve Block Clinic
Albert Einstein College of Medicine
Bronx, New York
Attending Anethesiologist
Flushing Hospital & Medical Center
Flushing, New York
Attending Anesthesiologist
Flushing Hospital & Medical Center
Flushing, NewYork

A BRIEF HISTORY OF TAOISM AND
THE HEALING ARTS
by Stephen Pan, Ph.D.

For many centuries, meditation and special exercises forms have been used by the Ancient Chinese, Hindus, Arabs, Jews and Christians as a means of improving the human mind and body. In China, the Taoists called it "Chi Kung," or "Cultivation of Energies." According to Taoist classics, Tu Hse, who lived about 8,000 years ago, was the successor to many great pre-historical sages. He was the great Taoist sage who began the use of the eight kua of the I Ching such as the great power of observation and the power of simplifying obscure masses of material. This resulted in a most perfect yogic and meditational form, which incorporated the insights of Tao philosophy.

Perhaps it is more than a coincidence that the Indian practice today of Kundalini Yoga is somewhat similar to the Taoist "Chi

Kung.'' More than 2,000 years ago, the Indian Master Bodhidharma traveled to China. There he meditated for nine years facing a wall at Shao Lin Temple. He established a school, which incorporated the Indian practice in a new manner. From the time of the founding of this school, many Chinese men of great ability practiced meditation as taught by this Indian Master and gradually applied to it the perticular qualities of the Chinese culture.

These esoteric practices were an integral part of the development of Chinese medicine, where acupuncture, herbology and other aspects of what would now be called ''holistic'' medicine reached a state of high refinement unsurpassed by any other early civilization. But by the end of the fourteenth century in China, these arts were in decline for various political reasons, causing many of the teachers to be scattered from their schools and forced to go under ground.

The various approaches have been compiled in a Chinese Taoist encyclopedia that fills hundreds of volumes. The Taoist approaches have been divided into more than ten branches of study, some of which have very different methods of practice ranging from breathing techniques to alchemical secrets.

Western medical researchers are just beginning to realize the ancient masters understood profound aspects of the human mind and body without the aid of sophisticated diagnostic machines. The difficulty is in penetrating the veil of secrecy drawn across these Chinese practices which prevents their open examination by the modern medical community.

Mantak Chia is one of the first Chinese masters to arrive in the west with a comprehensive mastery of both the traditional chinese healing arts, diet, Five Elements nutrition, herbs, Tai Chi Chuan, massage, moxibustion — as well as the esoteric arts of Chi Kung, Healing palm, Five Finger Kung Fu, Seminal and Ovarian Kung-Fu, and the meditative aspects of taoist yoga.

Chia is heir to a secret method which has been passed down by word of mouth only. Unlike his forebears, he feels that it is time that what he has learned should be made public. In the book he has attempted to simplify what he has learned by way of his own experience and those of his students into a system in which traditional and modern medicine are fully integrated.

The medical applications of the chinese esoteric system are traditionally said to be extensive, and include remedies for a side range of illnesses:

1. Asthma and Chronic Bronchitis

2. Rheumatism and Arthritis

3. Hypertension

4. Insomnia

5. Cirrhosis of the Liver

6. Pulmonary Tuberculosis

7. Recurrent Headaches

8. Frequency of the common cold and other Episodic diseases

9. Tumors

Long-term diligent practice beyond two years and, most effectively, if practiced life-long, reportedly could retard the various degenerative changes associated with old age e.g. skin changes, senility, slowed reaction time, impaired memory, ambulatory impairment and the frequency of various diseases common at old age.

A diligent practioner often lives to ninety years of age and remains healthy and alert, is able to jog, run and climb mountains with ease, and continues to enjoy life more fully than most people. Many reportedly could forecast their own time of death and pass on peacefully and gracefully in the posture of meditation.

However, it should be noted that in old China your doctor was considered a failure if you became sick. The best doctors trained their "patients" to prevent illness by maintaining a high level of health. The promise of Esoteric Taoist Yoga is to reveal the methods bringing your various bodily energy systems into harmony.

STEPHEN PAN, Ph.D.

Dir. East Asian Research Institute

New York, N.Y.

A DOCTOR'S SEARCH FOR THE TAOIST
HEALING ENERGY
by Lawrence Young, M.D.

When I was twelve and had just begun my grammar school education in Hong Kong under the British system, I was at an age of fantasies and hero worship. I was crazy about physics, mathematics, atomic bombs, hydrogen bombs and nuclear reactors. Albert Einstein was my hero and I wanted to be a physicist, discovering the smallest particles of energy and matter, while exploring the galaxies and the ever expanding universe.

Oddly enough, it was during the same time period that I read about the esoteric experience of Master Yun. It was written in Chinese, and I had the good fortune of having been taught how to read classical, modern and simplified versions of the chinese language. I did a lot of reading, staying in school and public libraries in Hong Kong several hours a day after school was over. There I read about Master Yun's strange experience.

Master Yun was 28 in the year 1900. Pulmonary tuberculosis was rampant in his village. Many villagers had died, including his cousin. Then he came down with a cough which lingered for several months. One day he coughed up a large amount of red blood and went into a panic. He checked with his village elders, as well as the traditional herbal doctors. They all confirmed that there was no treatment for pulmonary tuberculosis in 1900. Sunlight, fresh air and adequate rest were the only hope.

However, they did come up with an idea — the last chapter of the book: Annotated Chinese Medicinal Formulae recommended Taoist Meditation as the best form of adequate rest. It suggested that completing the Small Heavenly Cycle through the practice of Taoist Meditation might activate the bodily defenses powerful enough to overcome disease. Master Yun had practiced Taoist Meditation since his teens but without any significant effect, except that he always felt stronger when he practiced it regularly. Threatened by death, he read the methodology in the Annotated Chinese Medicinal Formulae carefully and consulted the village elders for clarification of certain details. Then he commenced practicing four times a day for two hours at a time, isolating himself in a small cottage.

On the eighty-fifth day, a sudden vibrating in his navel area caused heat to rush up his spine to the back of his skull. The same sort of vibration occurred on six consecutive nights with heat traveling up through his spine to the top of his head each time that he practiced. When it was all over, he seemed to have a new body. All symptoms of his illness were gone and he felt light and bright like never before.

One night, two years later, the vibration started up again in his navel. This happened on three consecutive nights. The vibration and heat rushed up his spine on its own, hitting the back of his head (at the occiput) and causing considerable pain. One night his skull suddenly felt as though it had cracked open and a sensation of heat swirled round and round in the top of his head. This began to happen every time he sat down to practice.

After another six months, a vibration again started suddenly in his navel and the heat again rushed up to the top of his head, swirled around in the vertex, came down his face, continued down to his chest and went on to again reach his navel. Thereafter, during every practice period, the heat went up his spine to the top of his head, then came down his face and chest and returned to his navel, after which, the heat circulated round and round without stopping. Master Yun remained healthy until his passing in his nineties, living a normal secular life.

I recount Master Yun's personal experience because his autobiography, first published in 1914, is an important landmark in Taoist Meditation. Before him, no one had written about the actual methodology, personal experience, benefits or side effects in simple, explicit language. There are volumes and volumes of Taoist Esoteric writing in Classical Chinese but the methodologies and accounts of experiences are hidden in a cryptic language. The benefits are written more explicitly, but the side effects are frequently clouded.

At age twelve, fascinated by the personal experience of Master Yun, I started to go through all the available Taoist classics that I could lay my hands on. But I was disappointed because I simply could not break what seemed to be a code, although I could understand every single Chinese word literally. It was then that I started an unending pilgramage to Taoist and Buddhist temples. I went to temple after temple but found that there was a lot of ritual, philosophy and religious data built into the meditation programs. Because I refused to do the rituals. I could not be initiated into Taoist practice. I was concerned by the fact that Master Yun had no teacher, he learned from a Chinese medicine book and was never initiated into Taoist practice via rituals. Never the less, I managed to talk to several Taoist teachers and many of their students, whom are now scholars and successful businessmen in Hong Kong, and was able to learn of their personal experiences in terms of energy flow and improvements in health similar to Master Yun's.

Initiated Taoists spoke of step by step guidance into the experiences that Master Yun had described and then higher levels beyond that. Master Yun had no such step by step methodology. He had only one step and one method that carried him through the experience described above.

Unfortunately, university life was demanding, and there were so many new attractions and distractions, that I stopped researching Taoist and Buddhist meditations after I entered medical school. The busy internship and residency years carried me even farther away from my investigations. My resurgence of interest began several years after my residency when I was in private practice. Although I was using every means available to modern medical science, many of my patients were still suffering and some of them continued to die, perhaps needlessly.

The memory of Master Yun's experience came up one day, along with the advice the many Taoist and Buddhist initiates and teachers I had seen. I had the thought, "If a patient has exhausted all forms of available medical care, he should at least have the right to try some safe mental techniques like meditation." I set out on a new pilgrimage to Yoga, Taoist and Buddhist meditation teachers, biofeedback and stress reduction programs.

Mantak Chia is one of the teachers I have met in my new quest. He is able to reproduce what Master Yun was able to do and goes beyond that, doing what the Taoist initiates can do as well. He is a Taoist initiate himself, but he does not include any of the Taoist rituals, religion, or philosophies in his program. A Christian by conversion, he is a doer, not a talker. He teaches his students solid steps without any high-sounding philosophy.

I have interviewed many of his students and I estimate that over 50% of his students who put a reasonable effort into their practice, open up the energy channels with vivid sensations and with noticeable improvements in health. The rest of them open the channels, without the vivid sensations, but with improvements in health. A very small number drop out. I have observed no side effects in his students, although all of them were prepared to meet all sorts of unusual bodily sensations. His students come from practically all walks of life, and many different races.

All in all, Mantak Chia is one of the few living heirs to the great Taoist tradition. He has access to the codes in the Taoist Classics. He is writing the Taoist Esoteric Encyclopedia in simple English for everyone, dispensing what had been secrets for centuries in simple, solid, easy-to-follow steps. Many other Taoist Masters and initiates may not agree with him for giving this esoteric knowledge so freely.

If used for the improvement of health and the treatment of illness, it is morally justified to disseminate this knowledge far and wide. Fortunately, Chia refuses to teach higher levels of achievement that might lead to paranormal abilities, unless the student can prove himself to be a law-abiding and trustworthy citizen, willing to serve mankind and use his or her esoteric knowledge to help the needy in a selfless and generous manner.

I wish Mantak Chia every success in his ambitious endeavor.

Lawrence Young M.D. is an internist in private practice in New York City. He is the Director of the National Clearinghouse for Meditation Relaxation and Related Therapies and publisher of it's National Report.

CHAPTER 12

PERSONAL EXPERIENCES WITH THE MICROCOSMIC

CHIA: When I first came to the U.S. I practiced acupuncture. In time I discovered that many of my patients had been referred to me by a doctor, who, was interested in Chi Kung. Whenever he had problem patients who didn't respond to conventional western medicine, he sent them to me. Many of them responded quite well to what I had to offer. Now I've been in this country for about four years and it was at least two years before I met the good doctor. He was excited about the way many of his referrals had responded. He asked to interview my students, half of which were his patients. I agreed and in time he published a book called "Reports of the National Clearinghouse for Meditation, Relaxation and Related Therapies", his aim being, to interest the American Medical Community in what he called, "Investigative Reports" regarding meditation in relation to physical and mental health. (This report can be obtained by writing to: National Clearinghouse For Meditation, Relaxation and Related Therapies, P.O. Box 3184 Church Street Station, New York, N.Y. 10008)

The case reports were of people who had headaches for many years, others who had asthma and various other ailments such as allergies, insomnia, hypertension, stomach ulcers, constipation, heart problems, hemorrhoids, chronic fatigue, overweight and low back pain. Doctor Young feels quite confident that these methods will be taught here to doctors as part of their training within ten to twelve years. In fact, it has great promise in the field of preventive medicine and as a means of fulfilling one's potentials.

I offered a workshop at the American Holistic Medical Association's annual congress held at La Crosse, Wisconsin. Many physicians, nurses and holistic health professionals attended.

At this workshop was a nurse who had practiced the meditation of stilling the mind for four years. She reported that lately she had felt heat in her head, especially in her palate. Sometimes during practice periods, her tongue seemed to automatically reach up and touch her palate, at which time a shock would run through it. This greatly frightened her. During the workshop she learned that the tongue acts as a bridge that connects the two channels completing the Microcosmic Orbit. That night she practiced again and felt so full of energy that she continued to practice without getting any sleep and yet felt very energetic throughout the next day.

During three workshops, four participants successfully completed the Microcosmic Orbit and many others indicated the potential to do so in the near future. One physician had practiced T.M. for about ten years and had already begun to experience heat and light in his head during his T.M. meditations. By learning how the energy flows and placing his tongue to his palate during this training period in La Crosse, he completed the orbit. By concentrating on his navel he experienced the light flowing in his Microcosmic Orbit.

At the end of the seminar a number of physicians were of the opinion that the concept of the Microcosmic Orbit as being a continuous circuit of energy is more reasonable than one in which the energy is allowed to flow only up to the head or be given no direction at all as in certain yoga practices.

The following are taped recorded excerpts from workshops on the Microcosmic Orbit held in New York City, Boston, Boulder, San Francisco, Los Angeles and Tampa. Participants (identified here as "students") were asked to describe their experience with the Microcosmic Orbit. Responding are Mantak Chia and instructor Gunther Weil.

STUDENT: I practiced the Microcosmic Orbit every morning. The total time that I spend each day is one hour. I feel sensations of heat flowing through my body. Sometimes there are sensations of a cool kind of energy. Sometimes I feel as though my abdomen is filled with energy. I have spontaneous movements when I practice. When they first occurred I wasn't sure as to just what was happening and I found that I could stop them. When I relaxed, however, it started again, and I decided that it was generated from my body rather than by any choice of mine.

CHIA: This sort of thing is not unique to this system. Practitioners of yoga and zen and T.M. have all had similar experiences. The specific gyrations are unique unto the individual and to a particular time and place. However they are indentically produced when areas that block flows of energy resist and then open up.

STUDENT: If I don't have a half hour to practice what can I do?

CHIA: The Microcosmic Orbit can be practiced anywhere, anytime, even just for one minute. You can do it for even just half a minute. Just think a smile and relax down. I want to stress that at any time during the day that you find you have just one minute you should smile and relax down to the navel. Doing this, you will find that the microcosmic orbit is set into motion. If you collect those spare minutes you may be surprised at how much time you have practiced during the day.

STUDENT: Do you have to go through all the organs?

CHIA: No. At this point you should simply smile and relax and fill your heart with love, let the loving energy spread throughout the whole system. In the beginning you just have to go through each organ as you have learned. Just like you learn the A,B,C's in the beginning. When you practice more it becomes a part of you, and you can read quickly. In the same way, once you practice, when you smile it will quickly fill all the organs and glands with smiles and love. You should then feel as though something is going down into your abdomen. When you can sense something around your navel concentrate there and in moments you will feel the circulation begin.

The microcosmic orbit is important because it teaches you how to allow the mind to direct your blood circulation. The heart is the sole mover of blood in ordinary people. Here, we do Taoist Chi Kung. This is a means of mixing energy into the blood and is achieved by mind power. When this is done, the heart doesn't have to work as hard. If your hands are cold you should now be able to direct Chi there to warm them, because your mind directs the flow of energy and the blood follows. The more your mind is used to circulate Chi, the faster and easier your blood flows. If you jog or exercise violently you can increase your rate of circulation but here you can sit down and relax and though your heart doesn't work as hard as it normally does, your circulation will be increased.

STUDENT: I was born in New York. I'm an acupuncturist and I also teach people special corrective exercises based on a system by Master Oki from Japan. I do nutritional counseling, as well. I've been studying martial arts for ten years. I did Japanese style karate for three years and Shun Ryo and now I do Tai Chi. I also do some Kundalini Yoga. The first thing I was really fascinated by was the diagnostic power of this during the relaxation part when we were going down vertebra by vertebra. I could actually detect what went on there, whether it was compressed or irritated or collapsed or bent. I was really surprised. Then when Master Chi put his hand on me it was like someone had lit a match there. The whole thing was on fire even long after he'd touched me. The heat had gone into my lungs and I could feel it healing them. I'd had some trouble with my lungs previously. This training has made me more relaxed so that I can now deal with stress conditions much more successfully. I feel centered now and I have developed a considerable amount of self-assertiveness.

STUDENT: I have a hard time making the spiral in collecting the energy. Usually I feel that it overlaps or is of a distorted shape. I can't seem to make it spiral out.

CHIA: That's alright. That's the way it is in the beginning. Actually, if I feel I've done it incorrectly, I just do it again. Collecting the energy in the navel is so important.

We have two major divisions in our bodies. One consists of the heart, lungs and the brain, and the other part is the lower abdomen. The body can also be divided into hot and cold. Above the navel is heat and below is coolness or cold. That's why the Six Healing Sounds and The Fusion of the Five Elements are so important. There are some places where you can store energy without any harm, like the navel area, but when it accumulates elsewhere, it can cause unpleasant effects. You can compare concentration to bringing together into one point the sun's rays with a magnifying glass. Here we are able to add to that the ability to circulate that heat throughout the body. This will help your blood get warm and make you stronger and healthier . . . gradually feeding your body and then your soul and finally your spirit. Each level that you ascend to is altogether different. Your present energy is derived from your organs . . . but is still in a raw state.

The second level harmonizes these energies in the Fusion of the Five Elements . . . in which the heart, kidney, liver, lung and spleen are involved. Each of these organs produces its own particular energy and it is at this level that these energies are blended, or, as the name indicates, fused and then distributed throughout the body wherever they are needed. So when you don't collect the energy at the end of your practice you have no way of knowing where that energy may be stuck. If Chi has collected in your head or chest you may be in for a lot of trouble because your brain is very sensitive to heat and you may have terrible headaches and possibly delusions. When your heart overheats, you find that you can't breathe well and that it beats too quickly. In regard to this there is a rule in Tao which is to keep your head cool and your feet warm.

STUDENT: Why does the right hand have to be over the left?

CHIA: It has to do with Yin and Yang. The right hand is Yang and the energy flows from Yang, right hand, to the left hand which is Yin. You get more energy that way.

STUDENT: Does it make any difference if you are right handed or left handed or a man or woman?

CHIA: No. The hand position is the same for everyone.

STUDENT: If men gather the energy together at the end of a practice session first clockwise and counter clockwise and women abide by the reverse procedure, why aren't their hands reversed as well?

CHIA: The flowing of energy through the hands is the same. The circulation of energy through the cycle for the man starts at the head, and the energy circulation for woman starts from the earth. When the energy is yang to yin it's the same in both.

STUDENT: If a person is mentally unstable, is he going to be able to complete the Microcosmic Orbit?

CHIA: Some people come to me and after we talk I tell them to go see a psychiatrist. They are "too hot" and have to do therapy first to slow down. I let them know right away that they are not ready now.

STUDENT: Can the Microcosmic Orbit be used to aid in the relief of major medical ailments?

CHIA: Many people in this practice fall in love with their organs and quickly give up bad habits as a natural course of events. Those habits just don't appeal to them anymore.

I have a student in New York who completed the Microcosmic Orbit. One day he had pain suddenly in the back caused by a kidney stone and had to go to the hospital. At the hospital he was given an injection of morphine, which he later said felt just like the experience when the energy suddenly rose up to the head. Naturally he was excited and he called me and asked me if that was possible. I explained to him that this phenomenan lately seems to have been backed by scientific investigations into the way the body makes endorphins, which are morphine-like compounds, and how acupuncture works to stop the pain. Anyway, whenever he gets pain now he stops it by meditating. You have to have some idea of the magnitude of the pain that kidney stones can produce to really appreciate this account. That student never fails to thank me now.

GUNTHER: Often when we have workshops there are people who have had injuries in the back, knee, scrotum. When they do the microcosmic orbit they say they feel heat or pain in those areas, because the chi is going to those areas first to heal them. This is sometimes a little painful. It's like a resistance coil. The electricity flows and meets with an obstruction and takes a while to work through it. But then it works quickly. If you do it everyday you'll find a lot of healing in your body. Old injuries will heal themselves faster.

STUDENT: I've benefited greatly from the practice. I came here because I have an injured back, as of three years ago. I'd been treated by chiropractors, acupuncturists and masseurs in Taiwan and in Tokyo, but nothing helped. Then a friend recommended that I come here because she said that she had had good results doing your meditation. After I had practiced about six weeks, I awoke one morning and felt a flowing sensation rise up through my legs.

GUNTHER: You'll have different experiences at different points. Some points won't have any sensations at all. And other points will be very st. It changes all the time. It depends on your general state of health that day, the atmosphere, how much prior experience you've had.

STUDENT: From doing the microcosmic orbit and the Six Healing Sounds I have a distinct sense of vitality, both physically and mentally. I find it an extremely valuable and valid approach. My first experience with meditation was in yoga and then, about 8 years ago, I learned Tai Chi and different types of meditation. Many teachers talked about energy flow, especially as regards to Tai Chi, but I never experienced it. I'd had my tongue to my palate through all of them, too. But this meditation here has created a sense of rooting that goes way beyond anything I've ever had before. What I'd heard years ago about such things was purely conceptual but what I get out of this meditation is an organic relationship between myself and the earth. I really feel as though I were like a tree rooted in the earth or a wave in the ocean.

The Six Healing Sounds have been very invigorating, too. Whether I do the orbit or the sounds I come away feeling the same. You can feel the energy move through the various pathways. It's a very distinct, definite sensation. You don't imagine these other pathways besides the Microcosmic Orbit. And those sensations are also clear cut and definite. Afterwards I feel very good; I feel more alive, I feel very peaceful. Then, during the day, I find that I have more energy and I feel very springy inside. I'd done Tai Chi Chuan for some years and I was concerned about hurting my knees in certain postures. After I'd practiced the Microcosmic Orbit for a few weeks I found that I was no longer troubled. What I assumed were knee stressing postures no longer troubled me.

STUDENT: I've had quite a lot of experiences doing the microcosmic orbit. The first four or five weeks I didn't feel much at all and I began to feel concerned. By about the sixth or seventh week I had sensations that were almost like an orgasm and then I developed a feeling of euphoria. As I continued to practice I felt the energy rise. For a while it remained fixed at the mid-brow area. In fact, I'd inhale when I practiced that was the only spot I'd feel. The most amazing experience I had was very recent when I was meditating at work. My tongue began to vibrate. My teeth then rapidly beat together and my head shook and then my body shook and my hands seemed to levitate upward. Then I realized that I could control the vibrations, at which point my body shook very fast, and then I slowed it down. This happens whenever I practice, now. It starts in the space of five or six breaths. At the end of such a session, I don't feel tired at all and that's what is most amazing to me. After I finish I bring the energy to the Tan T'ien and rotate there and I get very calm, relaxed and happy, and strong, too. Along the way I've had other sensations, too, such as a different taste in my mouth. It's great!

CHIA: That is very, very good. That taste you had, we call nectar, and that feeling of orgasm we call self-intercourse.

STUDENT: I've practiced acupuncture for about three years and have studied martial arts as well. When you passed energy to me I felt a wonderful feeling in my chest and insides that was incredibly expansive, and hot and cold at the same time. I had a feeling of well being, of being grounded.

GUNTHER: Each of you has to find the balance between staying at one point long enough to experience the energy gathering there and then wanting to go on by itself, versus going from point to point with your own mind because you're distracted. Only you can know which is best for you. The mind's always jumping around and wanting to do things and so if it's given a task to go point to point, sometimes the mind just wants to do it. If you sit and decide that you did this point and now you'll do the next, it's artificial. There's an internal balancing that has to happen. You have to do it till you're satisfied, deeply satisfied that you've done it. So at the beginning of this practice when you're alone at home or working, go slowly. Take 10 to 15 minutes on each point. Really exhaust it, deplete it. Sometimes the energy will go ahead. Sometimes it won't. Sometimes I don't notice anything. Sometimes I'll sit and I won't experience any energy at all but I'll feel the benefit of the practice. About 20% of practitioners of this don't experience the sensations but receive enormous benefits from it.

CHIA: Sometimes your vitality or energy is too low and so your energy doesn't seem to do anything. Usually each month you have a week or two of lowered energy but the more you practice these dips in energy will be evened out.

STUDENT: How are Tai Chi and the Microcosmic Orbit Related?

CHIA: Tai Chi Chi Kung takes the principle of the microcosmic orbit and puts the energy in motion. In other words it adds chi or internal energy to the Tai Chi movements and works on the tendons, the chi passing from the internal organs out to the rest of the body including the fascia, tendons, muscles and bones. The microcosmic orbit creates the energy that is then used in Tai Chi. You can't imagine how happy it will make you.

G. WEIL When you do the first level in this system you begin to regulate your energy, opening the main channels. In saving and regulating the energy you're beginning to balance it, but you still can't do very much with it. When you're assailed from the outside by factors that affect you emotionally you'll simply respond as you've learned to. That's why it's necessary that you do the first part of the Fusion of the Five Elements, because you learn a means of transforming the energy of your emotions, including anger. When you are in the presence of someone who's angry you can learn how to take that anger in and use it, or take your own anger and use it, by taking the energy out of the anger. Anger can be converted to a neutral energy either by returning it to its organ of origin (the liver) or by mixing it with the emotions of the other elements until no single emotion is any longer dominant.

STUDENT: I'm a chiropractor and I teach Touch For Health. This exercise was very powerful. The energy started going up my spine, like a jack hammer forcing its way up. When it went to the base of my skull my whole body shook. Then it went to my head, then my hair line, then settled in the bridge of my nose where it was really painful. Finally it felt like the energy went through. It moved down to the navel creating a huge amount of white light energy. A very powerful experience.

CHIA: Good. Keep your practice going every day. If you don't, all the energy will be reabsorbed. Just relax down to your navel and when you feel the navel is activated, go down to the next center, either the sperm palace or ovary center, and then to the perineum, and then to the coccyx. That is all there is to it. Remain there until the energy shoots up the back. Just keep the pump pumping up. The coccyx is like a pump that pushes everything up; and there's another pump at the upper end of the back, too, remember. Relax and smile down to your navel and the whole thing is set into motion.

STUDENT: How come you never gave us any preliminary exercises in breathing to do.

CHIA: Because you might have come to rely too much on it. Breathing is important, though, in establishing relaxation through the proper use of the diaphragm. Paying attention to breathing draws energy and attention from the mind and that acts as a drain and a distraction. Ultimately, we seek to arrive at 100% use of mind power and paying attention to the breath does not allow for that. Besides, on much higher levels breathing is no longer noticible. It is not without reason that we take as much time in letting everything "go down" so that the mind can be free.

There's something I'd like you all to understand. What you are practicing now is inner alchemy. The food you eat involves an outer alchemy. Many people today believe that by simply eating correctly the body will be brought to harmony. This is not true. If your body is not prepared your organs will not work together properly and all that good food will be wasted because it will not be utilized properly. It is common knowledge that under stress digestion and assimilation are hampered and that under extreme stress there can be an overall emptying of food contents. Of greater importance, then, is the cultivation of the inner alchemy. With no exaggeration, if the inner alchemy is balanced, the outer will take care of itself. In the higher level, when our bodies are in perfect balance, we can get along with little food, or no food at all.

STUDENT: Is it important for a husband and wife to meditate together?

CHIA: When you practice as a family you will all change, becoming more harmonious. I have a student who told me that whenever she concentrated on her navel in the morning and her husband moved his leg she could feel the energy in her own leg go into his. In a short time she observed that his overall health had improved and he was no longer burdened with frequent headaches and colds. Another of my students, Richard Wu, rid himself of his allergies through Taoist Yoga. When his wife found herself similarly afflicted she asked to learn the method so that she too could find relief. It took her just one day to complete the micro orbit. Her husband came to me pleased by her accomplishment but puzzled, too, because it had taken him months to do the same thing. I explained that that was not unusual and that their energies flowed in sympathy because they lived together and that being with a person who practices can lead to such results.

CHAPTER 13

AN M.D. INTERVIEWS THREE
PRACTITIONERS OF TAOIST YOGA
By Lawrence Young, M.D.

AN INTERVIEW WITH "S"

DOCTOR YOUNG: I would like to do an extended study of people who meditate. It's a venture that would call for a lot of follow up. Were you to take a drug for a month or so it would be fairly safe but were you to take it for 5 years it would not be. In the same way, the medical field is very eager to learn about poeple who meditate for a lifetime. That might include people who have problems, what the nature of those problems are, how they get problems and what they do to be rid of them. I'd like to know how you came to practice with Master Chia, whether there was any health problem that brought you into it or whether it was simply because you were interested in it.

S: It was a combination of all of them.

DR: Tell me about your health interest.

S: I hurt my back about 6 years ago and ever since then have a hard job sitting, let alone lying down. I couldn't sleep through a whole night, my neck especially would hurt me. Ever since I came to practice with Master Chia, in fact, immediately upon trying this, the pain abated. As though to prove the point, about 2 or 3 weeks ago I became a little slipshod about my practice. There seemed to be too many different formulae. There are formulae you have to do — exercises might be a better term — and I was pressed for time and began to find excuses. I cut down the number of repetitions that were called for in each of the meditations and, sure enough, my neck began to hurt again and my back has begun to hurt again, too.

I don't really know, it may be a purely circumstantial thing. There may be other factors involved in this case, but it would seem over the years that I tried various things and had no help. It is more than coincidence that when I tried Master Chia's practice it did seem to help. I had the usual orthopedic treatments with hot soaks and analgesics and muscle relaxants, which had me walking around in a stupor. I went to a chiropractor with very transitory results, but with some arrest of pain. Then I went to an acupuncturist, who didn't help at all. I then went to an herbalist who helped a little. This practice seems to have done something, seriously.

DR: What was the diagnosis?

S: They said that there was severe muscle spasm — especially of the upper back, involving the neck and the area that was subscapular. They also found a portion of my lower back in which the distance between the vertebrae was narrowed. It looked as though I'd have a chronic condition mainly because of some pulled or torn muscle attachments. For almost two weeks after I fell, I couldn't lift my head. Nothing would happen. No inkling of a message (that I wanted to lift my head) would come through. In fact, when I tried to get up, just after I fell, I couldn't. When I pushed myself over onto my side my head just flopped over. Gradually, after two weeks strength came back into my neck muscles, but there was still an assortment of clicking and crunching noises and pains. My head was tilted to one side and one shoulder was contracted and higher than the other for months. The insurance people, in fact, agreed that the whole area was in spasm.

DR: What did Master Chia suggest you do to cure this condition?

S: He first asked me to relax the area between and around my eyes. That alone helped to heal everything. All kinds of heat and flowing sensations came on on their own. There were various prescribed exercises designed to open up various energy routes. For example, the six healing sounds I found most relaxing. One is advised to do them before going to bed because they are conducive to good sleep. If I slowly stretch in the prescribed manner, allowing for the effects to become evident after each time, I very definitely loosen up. My pulse beats differently, I seem to throb all over. It has a very quieting effect. Really! Another favorite of mine is also soothing, though in another way. All that it consists of is gazing at a spiral-like diagram until my eyes begin to water and then closing them and rotating them a set number of times, first in one direction and then in the other. This produces a very good, soothing, soft, comfortable feeling. Again the area around the eyes to be very important.

DR: Basically, Master Chia taught a lot of relaxation exercises along with meditation?

S: I had developed a lot of tension doing the Micro Orbit and it was a matter of learning the knack of letting it happen that made the difference. Trying to do it interfered with it. First I had to learn how to relax.

DR: The experience of the Microcosmic Orbit is the main thrust of my investigation. There is a sensation of energy isn't there? Of course, it's not proven and it will be disputed by scientists in the medical field for some time to come. Tell me whether you felt it was real or imaginary and if there were any side effects from your practice.

S: I have been with Master Chia for nearly six months now. I can direct the power to flow in the microcosmic orbit and still not suffer any ill effects. I used to have a lot of heat in my belly and a ringing in my ears as a result of other spiritual practices I tried. Master Chia said that the heat and ringing of the ears should go away as a result of my practice with him. Heat, he explained, is an extreme. He advised me to mix cold chi energy with it and cool it down. I think this helped me to avoid a lot of side effects.

DR: Do you have warmth left?

S: I can produce it if I want.

DR: Did Master Chia give you energy or did you get it yourself?

S: I don't know. He said I could get it just by being at his center.

DR: Then he didn't do it more conspicuously?

S: No.

DR: Did he ask you to bring the heat in the Tan T'ien (lower stomach) up the back?

S: Right.

DR: Do you think you use your mind to guide it and therefore it's there? Is there a way for you to tell if it's imagination or not?

S: This approach does involve guiding the energy to wherever you've been asked to. It's done mentally because where the mind goes that's where all sorts of physiological effects have their origins.

DR: And how do you feel about that?

S: The method was suggested and I found that it wasn't difficult to do. I can feel the heat in my belly and if I think it's going to my back in the area of the Ming-men, it does and when I think-feel it's going up the back it does.

DR: If you don't try to guide it, will it also rise up the back and flow by itself?

S: Sometimes it does.

DR: Would you say that those times would give you some clue that your imagination is not needed?

S: Well, I did something in the beginning that he later told me not to do and that was, after the route was established, I let it go by itself and I wasn't concerned about the points along the way.

DR: That would mean, then, that you have to guide it continually.

S: I'd just let it go by itself and the energy just seemed to zoom around along the route.

DR: How long have you practiced?

S: About 6 months.

DR: How many minutes a day did you practice?

S: Maybe three quarters of an hour each time, twice each day. I've been told that I don't have to cycle the route as many times as I had. Originally, I'd been asked to do it 100 times which I never could because I'd lose count.

DR: How about the timing? How long does a cycle take? A second? A minute?

S: I can't say. It varied but it was not measured in seconds, because I had to visualize stations as it were along the way. Eventually, though, he had me just touch on four points at the navel, perineum, lumbar region and at the top of my head.

DR: What was the effect?

S: It was relaxing and felt warm.

DR: It helped your back?

S: Yes. I could sit in half lotus comfortably for a fairly long time.

DR: The muscles were relaxed. And Master Chia didn't suggest to you or have you autosuggest that you are healing your back?

S: No, though he did say that the practice would heal it.

AN INTERVIEW WITH DAN

Dan is a young photographer who, for eight years, had been putting much effort into practicing esoterics on his own, and had tried many other methods with many different masters. After studying with Master Chia for only two months, through simply concentrating on his navel, the Chi energy started to circulate in the Microcosmic Orbit automatically without concentrating on the other energy centers.

DR: I know that you have been studying with Master Chia for about two months. I would like to know why you came here in the first place and what you have found since.

DAN: I found out about Master Chia through the "Free Spirit", a magazine I picked up in a health food store. I called him up and he mailed me one of the booklets, which explains everything about the Microcosmic Orbit. After reading and practicing with forty to fifty teachers, his system sounded very good to me but I couldn't be sure and so I went to see him. After he explained the way the energy works, it seemed pretty logical to me, so I tried it out. He told me to concentrate on a point about 1.5 inches inside my navel, to feel warm — not to concentrate on anything else, to forget about breathing, forget about forcing anything and to just concentrate on the warmth in my navel.

DR: Did he say that you should make yourself feel warm, to create the warmth or just concentratre and to feel whatever you could feel?

DAN: First he taught me a breathing exercise to relax me and to get the energy in the navel going.

DR: So did the warmth come up by itself or you created it in your mind?

DAN: Actually I didn't feel much warmth in my navel. The other points felt warm, and my navel may have been slightly warm. I felt a lot of activity in the tip of my spine, in my back where my kidneys are, around my shoulder blades and especially in my head. My head felt, as though it had expanded and felt full of that same activity. My forehead and the tip of my nose felt numb. When I stuck my tongue up against my palate, I felt something like a charge of electricity on contact.

DR: You don't suppose that suggestion was somehow involved when he had you concentrate on your navel, do you?

DAN: No. I'd meditated myself for the past two years. Before I came here I had already seen yellow between my eyebrows, and had used it to concentrate on for hours at a time. When Master Chia asked me to concentrate on my navel, I saw light there too, but he told me not to pay any attention to it and insisted that I concentrate on my navel. In two days it had broken down to a yellow color sitting here and there and moving around but I didn't pay attention to it, I just continued to concentrate on my navel and kept my tongue sticking up toward my palate. I don't know exactly when, but I started to feel energy. My nose and my forehead grew very numb and I felt as though my head were expanding but he told me to just keep concentrating on my navel. Suddenly, I felt what seemed to be a vibration in the tip of my spine, in my back and between my shoulder blades, which after a while felt very warm, too.

DR: When did you feel that?

DAN: On Sunday, February 15, 1981 — the last time I was here.

DR: So for ten days you did not feel much of anything?

DAN: It was during my fifth session that I started to feel the energy.

DR: The other ten days you just felt a little bit warm in the navel?

DAN: The thing about it is that I feel the energy hitting my tongue sometimes then I can't keep my tongue in one place. It just shifts around by itself. I never had an experience like that before.

DR: What about your tongue?

DAN: I can't keep it in one place. It just moves around. This never happened to me before. The books I read, the "Mysterious Kundalini", "The Chakras", describe energy ascending up along the spine to the top of the head but Master Chia talks about it going all the way around and completing a whole route.

DR: You just concentrate on the navel and this energy surges up your back through your spine?

DAN: The first place that I felt something was in my back.

DR: How does it go from the navel to the back?

DAN: From the navel it goes down to the sperm palace and from there to the place between my anus and my testicles. I think he called it the perineum.

DR: Do you think you really felt it or was it because he told you about it?

DAN: I felt it but I wasn't sure at first. I also started moving around because I had been sitting too long and when I sat down again I also felt it. Now, I am trying to figure it out because I know it is real.

DR: You did not concentrate at the point in the back at that time?

DAN: No, only on the point inside the navel. Then it went up the spine and so on all the way around.

DR: How long do you think one cycle took you?

DAN: I can't tell exactly how long it takes.

DR: So basically you feel the point sensation rather than the current?

DAN: I feel vibration, even though I have felt heat but it moves like a vibration coming up.

DR: Is it through the point or in between?

DAN: It is more as though it is inside the spine.

DR: How about in the head?

DAN: I feel very good in my head. It feels numb and expanded.

DR: Do you feel a vibration going through it?

DAN: Yes, that's the numb feeling.

DR: But not like a river going through it?

DAN: No, I feel warm and at the end of the meditation I feel my head getting big and warm. I also feel as though something were moving very fast all through my body.

DR: You feel another body vibrating or your physical body?

DAN: I felt as though another body came out of me and extended six to eight inches beyond my physical self. The thing I didn't feel too happy about, though, is the pain in my right arm from an old injury.

DR: This happened today?

DAN: Yes, whenever I concentrate on my navel, now, whether it's at home or in the subway, I feel the vibrations.

DR: You can also do that in the subway?

DAN: Yes, but if I find a quiet place I can concentrate more effectively. Oh! I forgot to tell you that when I concentrated today I felt a sensation in my ears as though something had opened up, a sort of tickling. Master Chia described that as the channels opening up.

DR: Do you know how he teaches other students?

DAN: What I like about this system is that it is so simple, a baby could do it. It is not complicated. Just concentrate.

DR: You mean that you never concentrated in your practice?

DAN: Maybe once or twice but I used to concentrate in the higher centers, the thyroid or the solar plexus.

DR: And nothing happened?

DAN: No.

DR: Did you know that he tells his students to concentrate on different points along the line?

DAN: He did tell me, too, to concentrate on the base of my spine, my back, crown, etc. But I don't have to concentrate point by point. It just happens.

DR: That is what is so important about your case.

DAN: The main point that he is concerned about is to have the energy circulate and to get the channel open and strengthen the tissues. It is not imaginary, because I can feel something going up right now.

DR: I know. It's very important. You never even tried to bring it around?

DAN: Before that, I meditated very intently for hours on the point between my eyebrows. He said that that probably helped me. When I came here I probably did the right thing and completed the circle by sticking my tongue up against my palate. But right now it is still hard to tell what will happen.

DR: Yes, at least you have developed something, but whether it is beneficial or not, we have to see in the future.

DAN: I hope to develop my health to the fullest.

DR: Do you have any health problems?

DAN: I strained my left testicle and I have problems with hemorrhoids.

DR: Would you say your practice is spiritual or physical?

DAN: It is spiritual, physical, scientific, technological and especially related to my body.

DR: And hopefully it will lead to an advance in medicine for years to come.

AN INTERVIEW WITH BILL

DR: Our interview today is basically concerned with meditation and health. First of all I would like to know your background.

BILL: I am 37 years old. I work as a bartender. I study acting but I don't work at it. I have some Yoga training and have fasted for two months on pure water. I came to see Master Chia with my sister, because somebody told me there was a Tai Chi school here. I was impressed by what he had to say. There was nothing wrong with me. I just wanted to use it as part of my Tai Chi. So far, though, I have just stayed with Master Chia's Tao method. I was perfectly healthy before coming here but I have benefitted from this training anyway. I feel that my practice has made me extra calm. Along with that it helps me in my everyday life of being in contact with people. I can be more relaxed.

DR: You mean you are more efficient and enjoy life more?

BILL: Yes, along with that I also work out in my exercise class and do weightlifting. I feel more grounded when I do this practice. I can feel the energy in my body and it is a very positive form of meditation. I meditated before but never to such a great extent with any other teacher. I learned it on my own, from what I read, from yoga. Master Chia's system compliments the meditation I have already been doing.

DR: You say you did some meditation from a book? What book was that?

BILL: I read about TM in a paperback book that is on the market, but I sat on my own even before then.

DR: Did you feel "energy" even before studying with Mr. Chia?

BILL: It is not a matter of energy. It's more like sitting in a kind of consciousness. I never developed Kundalini or the power, I never felt it. It was just a certain kind of awareness that I had, like, when I concentrated on my arm I just felt the skin on my arm. I just tried to feel the blood circulating, it was just a matter of awareness more than anything else.

DR: How long have you lifted weights?

BILL: I've been doing it about 6 months.

DR: You started it just after you began meditating with Mr. Chia?

BILL: Yes.

DR: Would you say weightlifting and meditation benefit each other?

BILL: Yes, definitely. It contains a lot of techniques that I find in weightlifting. It is a way of connecting myself to the power that enables me to make rapid gains in my lifting.

DR: You say you practiced this method with Master Chia and felt energy. Do you really feel energy?

BILL: Definitely.

DR: Not like before, right? Because before you said it was just like an awareness but this time it is not?

BILL: This time it is not. When I read your book I related to my class mates tremendously how they felt this warmth, the heat, the coolness, I felt all that. It feels like a surge of energy that I get, I can feel it going through me.

DR: How many months has it been now?

BILL: Almost a year, but I have been coming on and off.

DR: How long had you practiced this method before you felt this energy? When did you feel the heat?

BILL: I consider myself very lucky because I felt it right away, the first day. I actually felt something. That is what caused me to come back again.

DR: Did he give you the power? Did he put it into your navel or something?

BILL: I remember him touching me. I think I felt something but it was very slight.

DR: So there is no special arrangement in giving it to you.

BILL: He showed me how to go about it and I think he knows that I am able to grasp it easily.

DR: How long does it take you to feel the circulation of energy?

BILL: It happened the first day. He told me to concentrate on the navel and I started feeling it. I wondered when I was feeling it, was it imaginary or was I really feeling it? Before he told me about it, he drew me a diagram of how the energy goes. This, of course, helped me to locate the energy when I visualize it in my meditation.

DR: So did you resolve the issue as to whether it was imaginary or not?

BILL: It is real.

DR: There is another thing that might help you, Master Yun, who lived in the 1900's and had no teacher explored this by himself. There have been others too. There is one who presently lives in Taiwan. They don't have any guidance, which may be more dangerous but they did find the route of circulation.

BILL: I would be more afraid if I didn't know what I was getting into. It would keep me from going into it if I didn't have guidance.

DR: Now, about circulating the first route that you opened up. What was it? How was it? Where was it?

BILL: It's in the front and the back and I at first thought it was my imagination. Then I started having the same kind of feeling, in my hand and along with it comes a certain kind of warmth, which changes sometimes, sometimes it's warm, sometimes it's cool.

Now, I do the thrusting route as the second part of the meditation. I was just telling Master Chia that I can feel it, that when the energy pushes up to the head it just feels like somebody hit my head with a hammer. I feel like energy is going thru. I was debating in my mind whether it was imaginary or real and I decided that it cannot be imaginary because I could feel myself jerk and shake as it goes thru and causes pain, on my left side here, around the colon area. It was so painful that tears actually came to my eyes. After I finished, I went to my belt route, after which I felt much more calm.

DR: Those feelings could be sensations of energy, but from a medical point of view it would be very hard to prove. Did the energy flow along a certain route in your body?

BILL: The front route (functional) and the back route (governor). It goes from the navel to the bottom and all the way around. It does follow that route and it looks like energy too. I do feel energy with it.

DR: How about acupuncture points?

BILL: I feel them, too.

DR: How did you feel it? Did the energy slow down at those points?

BILL: Like in the governor route, I can feel certain parts of my anatomy. The energy stops at the big points, like the coccyx, the crown, the mid-eye brows.

DR: Is the belt route at the navel level?

BILL: Yes, the belt route starts at the navel area and goes to my left and left around again up to my solar plexus, heart center, throat, eyebrows, and crown. Then it goes up and comes down again to my waist, going from left to right.

DR: Do you really feel the 4-5 circle of the belt route?

BILL: I feel it when I guide it.

DR: The idea is that there is no one fixed route.

BILL: That's not so. I'm doing the belt route, now. Here, I go up the crown and my body in a spiral pattern, passing definite places like my navel, solar plexus and heart.

DR: Did the energy jump across any empty space anytime in your experience?

BILL: Yes. Sometimes I feel energy quickly go up in my thrusting route, all the way from my coccyx to my head. When I direct it down to my feet, I can feel the power flow out of my soles and make a half circle outside of me from my toes to my head.

DR: How about common colds?

BILL: Yes, everybody had the flu. About two weeks ago, I came down with it. But I went through it very quickly. People who have the flu take nine days or even longer to recover. For me it took something like three days.

DR: I have interviewed a number of people who have related similar accounts to me. There must be something to it. They claim to have fewer colds now that they practice with Master Chia and they also claim that they can drive the cold away within a short time.

BILL: I think it will be interesting to try to heal more sicknesses this way. The west should be ready for this method because, and this is my own observation, the American people are just beginning to notice the power that they have, the power (energy) around all of us, call it what you may, God, energy, whatever. They are slowly coming to realize that there is something more than just the physical.

PART V:

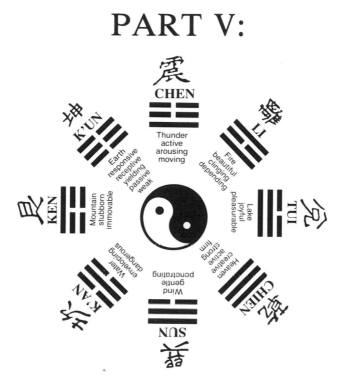

Beyond The Microcosmic

CHAPTER 14

OBSERVATIONS ON
HIGHER TAOIST PRACTICES

The following is a discussion by Mantak Chia on the higher levels of Taoist Esoteric Yoga, tape recorded at the annual retreat in North Andover, Mass. August 1982.

You endeavor in your practice here to open channels so that your soul has some place to go. The Microcosmic Orbit provides a crib for you, when you are a 'baby' so that your soul and spirit can run on it. As you grow up a separate room is made ready to provide you with privacy.

This room represents the 8 psychic channels. When you get a bit older you are provided with yet a larger room, the 24 channels. It is then that you are taught what is good and what is dangerous in the lesser enlightenment, the greater enlightenment, the greatest enlightenment, the sealing of the 5 senses and the congress of heaven and earth. You are 'six years old' now and in school. It is during this time that you acquire the ability to extend the spirit outside of you. At first you may be able to let it go out about one foot and then withdraw it. Gradually you can let it out more and more until after some time you can let it roam about freely outside of your body. This education of the soul and spirit is a tedious and time consuming process, taking 30-35 years.

There may be some geniuses who can become adept at astral projection in as little as 20 years, but there is always the risk that madness can ensue with premature exposure to forces that one is not yet ready for, madness of a sort that masters are afflicted with and must keep secret. I know, because I have met many troubled practitioners. In fact, M.D.s refer just such problems to me.

There are teachers who have had ill effects using their own particular methods, but still continue to teach because they adamantly maintain faith in those methods that they espouse in spite of how they have suffered by them. The methods should serve the practitioners. In this light, there is no Taoist method, but rather practioners who make of Taoist Yoga their own individual methods. Tao is a word that signifies the natural way of life. Each of you must find your Tao, open your channels and essentially make your system. When you are the least bit successful in this endeavor you will realize how truely priceless such knowledge is. You will learn how to pity the very people who might have caused you great anguish, as much by your own interpretation of their action as by their unwritten display of their own troubled minds.

In first level work we learn how to relax to a much deeper degree than we are ordinarily able to. Here we learn to 'smile' to the heart and to fill the heart with 'love' and then let that 'love' radiate throughout our whole system. You have to know how to love yourself. You have to know how to love your organs. If you can't love your organs or yourself, how can you be able to love others?

It is best that everyone in a household practice. Then they can all improve. If there is just one practitioner, he or she would probably find energy drained by others that one lives with. It is as though there were just one breadwinner in the house and everyone else is living off of him. Were they all to work, they would all share equally and all prosper equally.

The foundation for all subsequent practice is the microcosmic orbit, seminal ovarian kung fu, iron shirt chi kung and tai chi chi kung. Seminal ovarian kung fu is important in sealing the lower centers as the front door and the back door, the reproductive organs and the anus, to prevent a leakage of energy. The fusion of five elements prevents further leakage through the five sense organs. Iron shirt chi king is important in storing energy and tai chi chi kung helps bring energy to your hands and legs. You can see that what I teach is an entire system.

TAOIST YOGA AND THE KUNDALINI
by Michael Winn

Although Hatha Yoga became known in America in the 1930's, it was not until the late 1960's and 70's that attention began to focus on the higher stages of yogic development in which a phenomenon occurs known as "awakening of the kundalini". The kundalini is the sudden release of vast untapped reservoirs of creative energy that transports an ordinary human being into states of higher consciousness and bestows upon him or her unique creative powers. A person who has attained full command of this cosmic energy is said by the Hindus to have attained a state of "samadhi". The Buddhists call it "nirvana", while the Chinese refer to it as the "Tao". In the west it might correspond with what Freud alluded to as an "oceanic feeling", but among the prophets of the New Age it is known as "superconsciousness". None, of course, agree as to the best path to achieve this awakening, but the parallel among them is distinct.

In India, the kundalini is symbolized by a serpent awakening from a deep slumber and rising up from the base of the human spine in a spiralling motion through the seven energy centers (chakras) of the body, purifying and unblocking the powers of each center as it rises. For millenium this same serpent has been a universal symbol for wisdom and healing. Nearly every Egyptian pharoah is depicted in statues with a serpent emerging from the third eye in the forehead.

Today, modern western doctors wear on their white laboratory coats the Greek symbol of healing energy, two serpents spiralling up a staff. The taoists* in China revered the snake as a wise animal, but symbolized the Tao more abstractly, with the yin and yang symbols spiralling into each other. It is important to note the Taoist yin and yang spiral was contained within a circle, while the traditional Hindu kundalini serpent spiralled vertically up to the crown chakra atop the head.

*The Taoists referred to in this essay, are the masters of Taoist Esoteric practices, whose traditionally secret methods were studied by Master Mantak Chia. This is not to be confused with the Taoist religions, whose priests combined elements of Buddhism, Esoteric Taoism, and Chinese culture (folk beliefs, confucianism) in order to maintain a popular base.

The symbolic difference translates into a real difference in terms of the meditational approach aimed at awakening the release of this cosmic energy. The Hindu yogis emphasized raising the kundalini energy up to a higher transcendant level, while the Taoist masters emphasized harmonious circulation of this energy between chakras. The taoist emphasis was on achieving perfect balance between yin and yang forces within the body rather than on leaping beyond human form into divine states.

It was not enough for the Taoist masters to simply know that the Tao, the highest state of oneness existed; the problem was how to gain experience of it in a safe, systematic, verifiable, and useful fashion. Chinese pragmatism worked its way into Chinese metaphysics. One did not raise up one's consciousness toward Heaven without rooting it equally deep in the Earth. This need for "grounding" defined the development of Taoist yoga. Tai Chi Chuan is nothing more than a walking yoga with self-defense and healing applications. Unlike Indian yoga, one's feet never leave the ground, increasing one's "rootedness" in the earth energy and safeguarding against excessive kundalini energy in the head.

It is this excessive energy in the head that often leads to illusions of spiritual advancement, also known as spiritual egotism. It is not unlike an intellectual who spends all his energy arriving at conceptual solutions to the world's problems, but ignores the messages from his own body about its poor health or finances. In a similar vein, Wilhelm Reich once complained that yogis would often drive energies into their head chakras without removing the "body armor", or tension, plated about the lower body. He argued their heads would pulsate with higher energy, giving the illusion of cosmic serenity, but progress to full circulation of the cosmic energy would remain blocked.

The Esoteric Taoist system guards against this danger by beginning with the very lowest chakra energy, the survival needs, and constantly reintegrating it with the higher energies that are developed. The Microcosmic Orbit is a perfect example, as it circulates past all seven chakras in the body. Likewise, the Taoists don't advocate sudden abandonment of all one's ego. Depending on the individual, a secure job and loving family, may supply the best grounding for spiritual growth.

The Taoists advocate moderation, not asceticism. They teach that if a desire is destructive, it will drop away naturally as the body's chi flow comes into balance. The goal is to bring the body, mind, and spirit into harmony with the world, not to escape from it. Tradition has it many Tao masters would spend decades moving among the common people. Only after teaching them how to balance their anger with love, how to live more harmoniously, would they disappear up into the mountains to work on a very high level of meditation that required deep absorption in nature.

This harmonizing of the forces that fuse man, society, and nature together is evident in Chinese classics such as the I Ching. Written by esoteric Taoist masters, it simply expresses in poetic form the subtle changes in the balance of chi energies they observed in themselves, others, and nature. The proper approach to understanding the I Ching at its deepest level is to train oneself using Taoist esoteric yoga to read the changing elements within oneself.

In the higher levels of Taoist meditation the practitioner grounds him/herself in the body by channeling higher energies into the acupuncture meridian system, and circulating them throughout the entire body after refining the energies into a digestible form. The practitioner has a detailed map of the body's subtle nerve system into which he guides the released energy. He also is given precise methods for transforming his physical, emotional, and mental make-up at different stages of growth using this new energy. Each individual must tailor this "internal technology" to his specific needs and problems. Esoteric Taoism doesn't solve ego-created problems by demanding the surrendering of one's individuality to a larger group of guru.

The only devotion it demands is a disciplined committment to leading a healthy and harmonious life. Taoist Esoteric yoga is compatible with any religious belief. The language of Taoism is not defined by any set of mental "beliefs", but by the "experience" of increasingly subtle and powerful forms of chi energy. No mythological entities or divine symbols are evoked. But if someone chooses to identify this chi with the Christian notion of the Holy Spirit, it will not adversely affect the Taoist method of chi transformation. This holds true at the very highest levels of practice. This same Christian could draw accurate parallel between the Biblical ascent of Elijah on a flaming chariot into Heaven with the Taoist formula for the seventh stage meditation, "Reunion of Man and Heaven". Similar parallels could be drawn with Buddhist Hindu, or Qabalist symbols of spiritual advancement. The point the Taoist masters were making is that the pattern of chi flow and balance is similar in all men, regardless of interpretive beliefs about their religious experiences.

Taoist yoga is a theologically neutral method for preparing the dense physical and mental body to consciously receive a more powerful dose of cosmic yin and yang energies. Imagine the average human being is accustomed to functioning on 110 volts. He cannot suddenly absorb into his conscious mind the kundalini energy, which is powered by the subatomic nuclear energy that binds the universe together and is made visible in the radiant heat and light of the sun. To even double the received voltage to 220 requires considerable conditioning of the body. The more accessible form of Kundalini power is human sexual energy. But to absorb anything above your accustomed voltage is dangerous, like being struck by lightning without a ground wire to the earth. The Taoist system of circulating chi, from the Microcosmic Orbit up to the level "reunite Man and Heaven", is a grounding rod for Kundalini energy.

Modern researchers into spiritual phenomena see the Kundilini as a possible mechanism to describe radical leaps in the evolution of human consciousness. The form in which it spontaneously occurs (i.e., without special yogic training) in nature would produce, in successful cases of evolution, creative genius, and in the unsuccessful, madness. The classic account is Gopi Krishna's autobiographical "Awakening of the Kundalini" (Shambhala Press).

Gopi Krishna was an Indian railroad official who in 1937 experienced abrupt, dramatic physical and psychic changes as a result of his yoga practice. Energy began dancing and coursing powerfully through his body, but his initial wonderment and bliss soon faded. He was nearly incapacitated by it as the energy would not stop, sometimes leaving him tormented and sleepless for days on end. Only after twelve years of this nightmare existence was he able to learn how to balance the energy within his body and use it in a newly discovered creative life as a poet and author of a dozen books.

The Kundalini Research Institute in New York City reports worldwide over a hundred cases each year of individuals who cannot explain the uncontrollable release of energies in their body, often accompanied by days of sleeplessness, ringing and hissing noises in the ears and flashes of light inside the body. Some are students of yoga or meditation whose teachers abandon them after seeing they are powerless to diagnose or help the condition.

For this reason kundalini-oriented practices have earned a reputation as dangerous, radical, and unsafe for most westerners seeking what they falsely perceive as the fastest path to enlightenment.

A number of students suffering from kundalini-like side effects of different meditational practices have come to Mantak Chia for advice. Usually after doing the Microcosmic Orbit or simply putting the tongue to the palate and thinking down, these unpleasant symptoms disappear.

But the chinese esoteric system is not limited to therapeutic uses. Practitioners of other techniques, sitting, mantra, pranayama, can achieve a high level of awareness and a balanced experience of kundalini-like energies. But several have come to Master Chia and privately complained that they don't know what to do with all their energy, or how to transform it to an even higher level. One yogi wrote Master Chia that even after doing yoga for 18 years, 12 of them in an advanced practice of kundalini yoga, he had never felt such a "pure and distilled energy" as he experienced in the Microcosmic Orbit and first level of Fusion of Five Elements. He plans to integrate the Taoist yoga into his daily sadhana.

Another high level Zen meditator told Master Chia he felt alienated from the masses of unawakened human beings and depressed by the mechanicalness of their living only to eat, work, drink, and sleep. Master Chia taught him how Taoists harmonize with larger forces outside of the self.

At the very highest level Esoteric Taoist yoga has techniques to awaken the kundalini energy to such a level that consciousness is thrust beyond the body for the purpose of doing spiritual work in subtle realms of consciousness. According to Master Chia, the Taoist masters modified a crucial aspect of the kundalini yoga techniques learned from Indian masters who travelled to China. The Taoists detected a practical problem with the Indian method, which unites the human mind with its higher spirit by literally ascending out the crown chakra above the head.

If one ascended out the crown chakra prematurely, there were grave physical and psychic dangers. But if one took too long there was also the danger of physical death before one had completed the process of transforming mind and body energy into spiritual energy. The Taoist masters resolved this problem by incorporating their knowledge of subtle anatomy of chi flow. The result is that in Taoist esoteric yoga one does not focus energy on a single chakra, such as the heart, third eye, or crown chakra, with the intention of using that energy center as the gateway to higher consciousness. It is possible to open one or several higher chakras and still have their power undermined by physical or moral weakness in the lower energy centers. This can block progress to the highest levels if the practitioner denies or ignores this imbalance.

The Taoists avoided these problems by absorbing higher energy, whether from outside sources or sexual resources and circulating it continuously through all the centers. The goal was to build a solid and powerful energy base, self-contained within the human form, before the final transormation of the mind (or "soul") into spirit was effected. They would so thoroughly master their chi flow within the body that they could consciously circulate this chi outside the body as preparation for a safe pathway on which this soul could follow.

Master Chia thus describes the Taoist approach to kundalini awakening as the body and mind "parenting" the rebirth of its own soul into the next dimension of consciousness. One does not expect a human infant to fend for itself immediately after birth; that is the parent's responsibility. The reborn soul, ascending out the crown chakra and arriving as an infant in a confusing new world, would have "adult" guidance in the form of a powerful field of balanced chi energy protecting it from malevolent astral forces.

Because the full transformation of all physical and mental chi into spiritual chi energy normally takes many years, there is a danger of premature physical death before the process is finished. This danger becomes more acute with practices that accelerate the inrush of kundalini energy, as the body and glands must adjust to radical changes in metabolism. The Taoist masters circumvented this by mastering the act of physical longevity, chronicled widely in Taoist literature as the quest for physical immortality. The collective genius of the Taoist masters evolved an esoteric spiritual system designed to simultaneously awaken the kundalini and function as a healing system applicable to the whole gamut of daily stresses and illnesses.

The attraction of the Taoist yoga system is that it is as safe and methodical as climbing a ladder. You climb only as high as you can safely maintain balance and still keep the ladder rooted. The Taoist masters emphasized staying in harmonious balance on each step was more important than getting to the top of the ladder; trying to jump ahead increased the risk of falling. The goal was not to leap into some transcendent pie-in-the-sky, but to arrive with the graceful surefootedness of a Tai Chi dancer.

Awakening of the kundalini energy does produce a transcendent state of consciousness, but with Taoist Esoteric methods it is only achieved when the ever changing and opposing forces of yin and yang are first identified and then continuously, even automatically, brought into harmonious balance by the individual. It is a process available to anyone anywhere with a functioning mind, whether he/she is rich or poor, a cripple or an athlete, a housewife or an executive, a criminal in prison, or a sailor alone at sea.

This internal feeling of expanding harmony is the highest freedom available to human beings, but unfortunately is rarely sought for lack of vision or discipline. Taoist Esoteric Yoga is an ancient system that has proven its worth over many thousands of years in aiding seekers to awaken awareness of that highest harmony.

CHAPTER 15

SUMMARY OF THE SEVEN STAGES OF TAOIST ESOTERIC YOGA

SMALL HEAVENLY CYCLE
(MICROCOSMIC ORBIT)

The introduction to the seven higher formulas of Taoist Esoteric practice is the Opening of the Microcosmic Orbit, or the rebirth process of return to the mother's womb. This route is composed of the Functional and Governor Channels, which must be purified and linked to form a free-flowing circuit.

The life of a human being begins with the piercing of an egg by a sperm cell. From this original act of Kung Fu, an enormously complex human being develops, which is capable of real genius. The fetus develops around that point, which is called the navel. It is from this point that nutrients are absorbed and wastes expelled from the developing creature. Therefore, in the Warm Current Practice the navel is a point of overriding importance. While in the womb the human being doesn't breathe air (the lungs do not function at all). Energy and oxygen are passed to the fetus through the umbilical chord. When the energy flows into the fetus' body, it enters at that point at which the navel will later be after the umbilical cord is severed. Then it proceeds downwards to the bottom of the trunk, flows all the way up the spine to the crown of the head and from there, flows down the middle of the face continuing on to the navel, again to complete the circuit.

The fetus, it is said, automatically touches its tongue to its palate. This serves to link the two energy channels and allows the power to flow. The crown of the baby's head is open and moves up and down. This is due to the waxing and waning of the flow of power through this particular part of the body.

Thus, the tongue is the terminus of the Functional Channel. This energy pathway begins at the bottom of the trunk at the point midway between the anus and the testes, called, the "Hui-Yin". From there it flows up the front of the body through the Kuan-Yuan and the Chi-hai and then through the Chi-chung (the navel). Then it passes through the Chung-wan (solar plexus) and proceeds to the Shan-chung (the heart center). Thereafter, it passes through the Hsuan-chi (throat) center and up to the tongue terminus. When connected with the Governor Channel the energy path reverses direction and flows down from the tongue, navel, to the Hui-Yin.

The Governor (or control) Channel also starts at the Hui-Yin. From this point it moves up the posterior of the body. In doing so it passes through the Chang-chiang (the base of the spine) and goes up to the Ming-men (L2 and L3) or Door of Life where it continues up to the Chi-chung (T11) between the adrenal glands and then proceeds upwards to the Yu-chen or the Emerald Pillow of the medulla. From there it rises to the crown of the head or Pai-hui (the crown) and then goes to the Shen-ting and down to the Yin-T'ang between the eyebrows. Here it passes to the San Ken (the tip of the nose) and finally travels down to the palate, which is the terminus of the Governor Channel.

THE TONGUE IS A SWITCH OF THE CIRCUIT

The circuit may be closed when the tongue end of the Functional Channel is raised to contact the palate terminus of the Governor. Thus, during practice, we must keep the tongue in contact with the palate. Placing the tongue against the palate has a calming effect for those who practice the Warm Current Method. It also generates saliva, which is regarded as the water of life in Taoist practice. Saliva is said to be the chief lubricant of all bodily functioning. In the Taoist view the soft palate is regarded as a direct link to the pituitary gland.

As a man grows older he suffers increasingly from an imbalance of Yin (female) and Yang (male) energies in the body. As these disharmonies multiply, the bodily organs begin to suffer from the receipt of too much or too little energy. How different is the vital power of the infant! He grows nearly an ounce a day. This represents an astounding accomplishment in the assimilation of energy by the material body. The baby's body can do this heroic job of cell building because its routes of energy are thoroughly open and the flow of power is, consequently, very strong.

The Governor Channel controls the Yang organs of the body. These are the lungs, spleen, heart, kidneys, circulation-sex, and liver. The Functional Channel controls the Yin organs, which are the colon, stomach, small intestine, bladder, triple warmer, and gall bladder. The tissues are Yang in tendency and the blood is Yin.

THE SEVEN FORMULAS OF
THE SEVEN BOOKS OF THE TAO*

1. THE FIRST FORMULA:
FUSION OF THE FIVE ELEMENTS

This formula literally combines the separate energies of the five principal elements into one harmonious whole. The meditation has a particularly powerful filtering and purifying effect upon the human nervous system.

The Earth is the Mother of all the elements. All life springs from her generative womb. This reunites the other four elements of Chinese cosmogeny with the mothering Earth. Thus, metal, wood, water and fire are drawn back into the earth and are simmered gently at this point. Each element is purified but is not so hotly fused that it loses its integrity and dissolves into ashes.

This formula is regarded as a highly secret method of Taoist meditation. In Chinese Philosophy each element corresponds to a particular organ. The Earth corresponds to the spleen, metal to the

*The Taoist masters traditionally referred to each level of esoteric practice as a "book" with a formula even though, until now, they have never been written but passed down only by word of mouth.

lungs, water to the kidneys, wood to the liver, and fire to the heart. The five elements interact with each other in three distinct ways: producing, overcoming, and threatening. The producing or creating cycle runs thusly: wood burns to make fire, the ashes decompose and seep into the earth, where are born and mined metals, which when melted become water (liquid), which nourishes trees and plants. The overcoming or destruction cycle runs thusly: wood is cut down by metal, fire is extinguished by water, earth is penetrated by wood, metal is melted by fire, and water is interrupted and cut off by earth.

The life cycle also has its relative elements thus: birth corresponds to wood, growth to fire, maturity to earth, harvest to metal and storage to water. In climatic types, wind corresponds to wood, heat to fire, dampness to earth, dryness to metal, and cold to water. Their corresponding emotions (sympathy, sadness, joy, anger, fear) blend one harmonious whole, raising the morale and encouraging kindness, gentleness, rightousness, respectfulness and humor. The formula of the five elements combined into one involves the mixing of the Yin and Yang to attain a higher state of bodily harmony and beauty. The ancient alchemical formula SOLVE ET COAGULA corresponds to the second stage in the meditational forms.

In this stage you will realize the great use of the Five Elements which already exists in your body and which you may have studied but not understood experientially. The fusion of the elements, will provide you with such an experience. In this stage a cleansing of the whole body takes place. There may be much gas and bowel movements with very black, foul smelling stools.

Another six special routes must be opened, making eight routes in all. The first two are the Governor and Functional Channels. Next to be cultivated is the Chung-Ma.

The Chung-Ma, or Thrusting Route, which originates in the lower abdomen in the Hui-Yin and moves upward along two lines to the midpoint between the nipples where it spreads out to the shoulders and then joins at the collar bone. From there, it proceeds up to the face, crosses at the mouth and moves up to the point between the eyes and then up to the top of the head.

Another pathway of the Thrusting Route is started at the Yun-Chuan (the ground to earth), goes up the inside of the leg to the thigh and joins in the Hui-Yin. Starting at the Hui-Yin and running up through the center of the body, it passes through the large and small intestines, kidney, pancreas, liver, stomach, heart, lung, trachea, and up into the brain (pituitary, pineal and the middle brain up to the top of the head, Pai-Hui).

The second special route is the Tai-Ma. This energy channel originates at the ribs and circles the waist in ribbon-like bands. For this reason it is called the Belt Route. It is considered as a belt binding up the Yin and the Yang channels. This channel, when properly open, will spiral around the whole body. Looking down at the floor, the ribbon, as it were, would be seen to unwind going counter clockwise or right to left and proceeding up the length of the entire body, and joining all the body channels together. The spiraling is in a clockwise direction for women.

The third special route is the Yang-Chiao-Ma, the Positive Leg Route. It starts at the outer aspects of the two ankles and rises up the outside of the legs along the outer thighs. From the thighs it goes up to the hips, a strong absorbing energy center, the outer sides of the back and winds over the left and right shoulder, which are strong absorbing energy centers, whence it ascends along the neck to the corners of the mouth and enters into the eye-sockets and then over the forehead and skull to terminate in the medullar region.

The fourth special route is the Yin-Chao-Ma or Negative Leg Route. This channel originates at the center of the soles and turns along the inner sides of the ankles, rising up the inside of the legs. It passes from the inner thigh past the external genitalia and continues up to the chest, clavicle, throat and up to the face to the inner corners of the eyes. These routes are composed of two routes, one on each side and can be worked separately, also.

The fifth special route is the Yang-Wei-Ma. This starts at the front of the outer ankle and moves straight up the outside of the leg continues up the side, circles over the shoulder and proceeds up the side of the neck and face, over the forehead and skull, where it terminates in the medulla.

The sixth special route is the Yin-Wei-Ma. It starts on the inner shin and moves straight up the front of the body, over the knee, up the thigh, the side of the abdomen and chest and up to the nipples. From there it veers inwards towards the throat where it joins the Functional Meridian.

Thus, all of the energy passageways of the body are linked together in a network of the two Channels, the six special routes, and the twenty-four regular routes corresponding to the organs on each side. These passage ways are the superhighways, highways, and roads, respectively, of energy flow across the body.

2. THE SECOND FORMULA: LESSER ENLIGHTENMENT OF KAN AND LI

This formula is called Siaow K'an Li in Chinese and involves a literal steaming of the sperm (Ching) into life force energy (Chi). One might otherwise say that this begins the transfer of the power of the sexual hormones into the whole body and brain. The crucial secret of this formula is to reverse the usual sites of Yin and Yang power, thereby provoking liberation of the sperm's energy.

The first and second books are the preparation of the paths for the greater energy flow of the sperm so that the body will be able to handle the great influx of energy (power which might correspond to the awakening of the Kundalini). This formula includes the cultivation of the root (the Hui-Yin) and the heart chakras and the transformation of the sperm energy to sperm power at the navel.

This inversion places the heat of the bodily fire beneath the coolness of the bodily water. Unless this inversion takes place, the fire simply moves up and burns the body out. The water (the sperm and seminal fluid) has the tendency to flow downward and out. When it dries out that is the end. This formula reverses the normal, energy-wasting relations by the highly advanced method of placing the water in a closed vessel (cauldron) in the body and then cooking the sperm with the fire beneath. If the water (sperm power) is not sealed, it will flow directly into the fire and extinguish it or itself be consumed. This formula preserves the integrity of both elements, thus allowing the steaming to go on for great periods of time. The essential formula is to never let the fire rise without having water to heat above it and to never alow the water to spill into the fire. Thus is produced a warm, moist steam containing tremendous energy and health benefits.

The second formula consists of:

(a) Mixing of the water (Yin) and fire (Yang) (or male and female) to give birth

(b) Transforming the sperm power (generative force) into vital energy (Chi), gathering and purifying the Microcosmic outer alchemical agent

(c) Opening the twelve major channels

(d) Beginning of the half immortal (joining and sublimation of the body & soul)

(e) Circulate the power in the solar orbit (cosmic orbit)

(f) Turn back the flow of generative force to fortify the body and the brain and restore it to its original condition before puberty

(g) Gradually reduce food intake and depend on inner self, sun, moon and water, a beginning of the cosmic energy. (beginning of the Half Immortal)

3. THE THIRD FORMULA:
GREATER ENLIGHTENMENT OF THE KAN AND LI

GREATER YIN AND YANG MIXED I

This formula comprises the Taoist Dah Kan Li (Ta K'an Li) practice. It uses the same energy relations of Yin and Yang inversion but increases to an extraordinary degree the amount of energy that may be drawn up into the body. At this stage, the mixing, transforming and harmonizing of the energy in the Solar Plexus (it might correspond to the Manipura Chakra) takes place. The increasing amplitude of power is due to the fact that the third formula draws Yin and Yang energy from within the body, whereas, the third formula draws the power directly from Heaven (above) and Earth (ground wire — Yang and Yin, respectively) and adds the elemental powers to those of one's own body. In fact, power can be drawn from any energy source, such as the moon, wood, earth, light, etc.

The Third formula consists of:

a. Moving the stove and changing the Cauldron.

b. Greater Water and Fire mixed (male & female intercourse).

c. Greater transformation of sperm power into the higher level.

d. Gathering the outer and inner alchemical agents to restore the generative force and invigorate the brain.

e. Cultivating the body and soul.

f. Beginning the refining of the sperm power (generative force, vital force, Ching Chi).

g. Absorbing Mother Earth (Yin) power and Father Heaven (Yang) power. Mixing with sperm power (body) and soul.

h. Raising the soul.

i. Retaining the positive generative force (seminal) force and keeping it from draining away.

j. Gradually do away with food and depend on self sufficiency and Universal energy. (Breatherian)

4. THE FOURTH FORMULA:
GREATEST ENGLIGHTENMENT OF THE KAN AND LI
(T'ai K'an Li)

GREATEST YIN AND YANG MIXED II

This formula is Yin and Yang power mixed at a higher bodily center. This is to reverse the aging process, to re-establish the thymus glands to increase natural immunity. This means that the radiation of healing energy stems from a more powerful point in the body and provides vast benefits to the physical and etheric organism.

The Fourth Formula consists of:

a. Moving the stove and changing the Cauldron to the higher center.

b. Absorbing the Solar and Lunar power.

c. Greatest mixing, transforming, steaming and purification of sperm power (Generative Force), soul, Mother Earth, Father

Heaven, Solar and Lunar Power for gathering the Microcosmic inner alchemical agent.

d. Mixing the Visual power with the Vital power.

e. Mixing (sublimating) the body, soul and spirit. (True Breatharian)

This might correspond to the heart Chakra (Anahata).

5. THE FIFTH FORMULA:
SEALING OF THE FIVE SENSE ORGANS

This very high formula effects a literal transmutation of the warm current or Chi into mental energy or energy of the soul. To do this we must seal the five senses, for each one is an open gate of energy loss. In other words, power flows out from each of the sense organs unless there is an esoteric sealing of these doors of energy movement. They must release energy only when specifically called upon to convey information. This might correspond to the Brow (Ajna) and Throat Chakra (Vissuddha).

Abuse of the senses leads to far more energy loss and degradation than people ordinarily realize. Examples of misuse of the senses are as follows: If you look too much, the seminal fluid is harmed; listen too much and the mind is harmed; speak too much and the salivary glands are harmed; cry too much and the blood is harmed; have sexual intercourse too often and the marrow is harmed, etc.

Each of the elements has its corresponding sense through which its elemental force may be gathered or spent. The eye corresponds to fire; the tongue to water; the left ear to metal; the right ear to wood; the nose to earth.

The Fifth formula consists of:

(a) Sealing the five thieves: ears, eyes, nose, tongue and body

(b) Controlling the heart, and seven emotions (pleasure, anger, sorrow, joy, love, hate, and desire)

(c) Unite, transmutes the inner alchemical agent into life preserving true vitality

(d) Purifying the spirit

(e) Raising and educating the spirit, stopping the spirit from wandering outside in quest of sense data

(f) Do away with decayed food, depending on the un-decayed food, the universal energy is the True Breatharian.

6. THE SIXTH FORMULA:
CONGRESS OF HEAVEN AND EARTH IMMORTALITY

The sixth, most advanced, formula is difficult to describe in words. It involves the incarnation of a male and a female entity within the body of the adept (this might correspond to the Crown Chakra, Sahasrara). These two entities have sexual intercourse within the body. It involves the mixing of the Yin and Yang powers on and about the crown of the head and being totally open to receive energy from above and regrowth of the pineal gland to its fullest use. When the pineal gland is at its fullest, it will serve as a compass to tell us in which direction our aspirations can be found. Taoist Esotericism is a method of mastering the spirit, as described in Taoist Yoga. WITHOUT THE BODY, THE TAO CANNOT BE ATTAINED, BUT WITH THE BODY, TRUTH CAN NEVER BE REALIZED. The practitioner of Taoism should preserve his physical body with the same care as he would a precious diamond because it can be used as a medium to achieve immortality. If, however, you do not abandon it when you reach your destination you will not realize the truth.

The sixth formula consists of:

(a) Mingling (uniting) the body, soul, spirit and the universe (Cosmic Orbit)

(b) Full development of the positive to eradicate the negative completely

(c) Spirit returned to nothingness

7. THE SEVENTH FORMULA:
REUNION OF MAN AND HEAVEN.
TRUE IMMORTAL MAN.

We compare the body to a ship and the soul to the engine and propeller of a ship. This ship carries a very precious and very large diamond, which it is assigned to transport to a very distant shore. If your ship is damaged (a sick and ill body), no matter how good the engine is, you are not going to get very far and may even sink. Thus we advise against spiritual training unless all of the channels in the body have been properly opened and have been made ready to receive the 10,000 or 100,000 volts of super power, which will pour down into them. The Taoist approach, which has been passed down to us for over 5,000 years, consists of many thousands of methods. The formulae and practices we describe in these books is based on such secret knowledge and the author's own experience in over ten years of study and of successfully teaching hundreds of students.

The main goal of Taoists:

1. This level — overcoming reincarnation.

2. Higher level — the immortal spirit.

3. Highest level — the immortal spirit and immortal body, like a mobile house to the spirit and soul.

Chart of the Complete Taoist Esoteric Yoga System

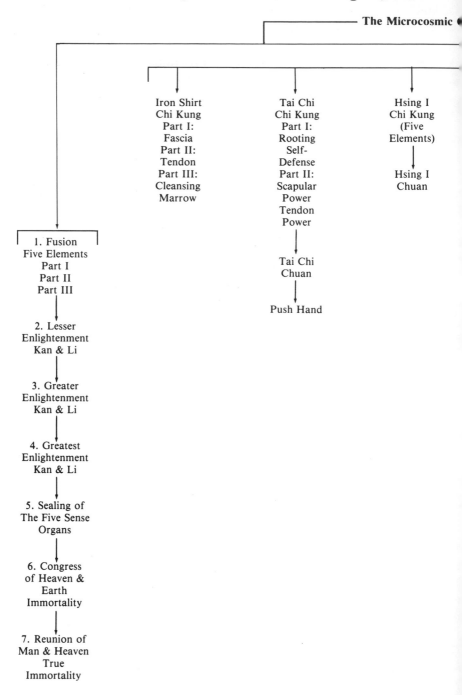

The Microcosmic

Iron Shirt
Chi Kung
Part I:
Fascia
Part II:
Tendon
Part III:
Cleansing
Marrow

Tai Chi
Chi Kung
Part I:
Rooting
Self-
Defense
Part II:
Scapular
Power
Tendon
Power

Hsing I
Chi Kung
(Five
Elements)

Hsing I
Chuan

Tai Chi
Chuan

Push Hand

1. Fusion
Five Elements
Part I
Part II
Part III

2. Lesser
Enlightenment
Kan & Li

3. Greater
Enlightenment
Kan & Li

4. Greatest
Enlightenment
Kan & Li

5. Sealing of
The Five Sense
Organs

6. Congress
of Heaven &
Earth
Immortality

7. Reunion of
Man & Heaven
True
Immortality

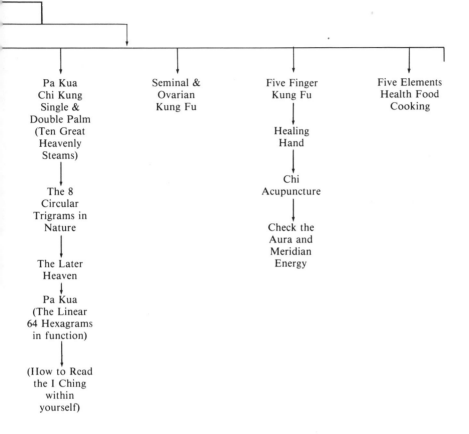

Pa Kua
Chi Kung
Single &
Double Palm
(Ten Great
Heavenly
Steams)

The 8
Circular
Trigrams in
Nature

The Later
Heaven

Pa Kua
(The Linear
64 Hexagrams
in function)

(IIow to Read
the I Ching
within
yourself)

Seminal &
Ovarian
Kung Fu

Five Finger
Kung Fu

Healing
Hand

Chi
Acupuncture

Check the
Aura and
Meridian
Energy

Five Elements
Health Food
Cooking

CHAPTER 16

TAOIST ESOTERIC YOGA
COURSE OFFERINGS

There are now 9 Taoist Esoteric Yoga Centers in the U.S. offering personal instruction in various practices ranging from the Microcosmic Orbit to Tai Chi Chuan, Pa Kua, Hsing I.

Taoist Esoteric Warm Current Meditation as these practices are also known, awakens, circulates, directs and preserves the generative life force called chi through the major acupuncture meridians of the body. At progressive stages, dedicated practice of this ancient esoteric system eliminates stress and nervous tension, massages the internal organs, and restores health to damaged tissue.

This practice is of particular use to practioners of polarity therapy, shiatsu, Kundalini yoga, Swedish massage and other healing arts in which the exchange and cirulation of life force energy — ki, prana or chi — must be maintained while working with clients or students. The first two formulas are described below. The remaining 5 formulas will be described when offered.

OPENING OF THE MICROCOSMIC ORBIT is the first level in the Taoist Esoteric Warm Current Meditation. Through unique relaxation and concentration techniques, it provides for purification of the first two major acupuncture channels of the body, the Functional and Governor meridians. Master Chia will assist students in the mastery of this technique by passing energy through his hands into their energy channels. (Course No. 1)

Completion of the Microcosmic Orbit is a prerequisite for any student who intends to study the higher levels of Taoist yoga which includes various forms of Chi Kung, Seminal and Ovarian Kung Fu, and the long and short forms of Tai Chi Chuan.

FUSION OF THE FIVE ELEMENTS AND CLEANSING OF THE ORGANS is the second level of the Taoist Esoteric Warm Current Meditation. At this level one learns how the five elements (earth, metal, fire, wood, water) and their corresponding organs (spleen, lungs, heart, liver, kidneys) interact with one another in three distinct ways: producing, combining and threatening. This formula combines the disparate energies of the five principle elements — and their corresponding emotions (sympathy, sadness, joy, anger, fear) — one harmonious whole. The filtering effect upon the entire psycho/physical system is particularly powerful as these combined energies circulate throughout the Microcosmic Orbit and the Six Special Channels.
(Course No. 9)

The second formula is taught in three parts.

Part I: The 12 steps for collecting, fusing, harmonizing and cleansing of the organs;

Part II: The opening of the three Chung-Ma (Thrusting-routes) and the nine Tai-Ma (Belt-routes);

Part III: The opening of the Positive and Negative Legs and Positive and Negative Arms.

THE SIX HEALING SOUNDS

This self-healing method uses simple arm movements and vocalizations to produce a cooling effect upon the internal organs. The Six Healing Sounds quickly eliminate stress, improve digestion, reduce insomnia and headaches and relieve fatigue. This method is useful to meditators as well as runners, practitioners of martial arts, and other intense exercise systems that tend to build-up excessive heat in the body. (Course No. 2)

CHI MASSAGE — TAOIST REJUVENATION

Using internal power chi and gentle external stimulation, this simple yet highly effective self-massage technique enables one to collect, and then direct chi to the sense organs and other parts of the body for self-healing purposes.

Taoist Rejuvenation dates back 5,000 years to the Yellow Emperor's classic text on Taoist, internal medicine. (Course No. 3)

IRON SHIRT CHI KUNG — THE HIGHEST FORM OF CHI KUNG

The physical integrity of the body is sustained and protected through the accumulation and circulation of internal power (chi) in the vital organs. This energy is stored in the fascia which is a layer of connective tissue covering, supporting or connecting the muscles or inner organs. Over time, the Iron Shirt Chi Kung practice strengthens one's vital organs as well as the tendons, muscles, marrow and bones.

Historically, the practice of Iron Shirt Chi Kung was a prerequisite to the effective study and eventual mastery of the various Kung Fu fighting styles. However, the main purpose of Iron Shirt Chi Kung is not for fighting; it is to achieve excellent health by increasing stamina and the body's ability to fight disease and defend its vital organs from unexpected injury. Prerequisite: Course No. 1 — opening the Microcosmic Orbit. (Course No. 4)

Iron Shirt Chi Kung is divided into three levels of instruction, I, II, and III. (See detailed description later this chapter.)

TAI CHI CHI KUNG — THE FOUNDATION OF TAI CHI CHUAN

Without the circulation of chi through the channels, muscles and tendons of the body the Tai Chi Chuan movements are only physical exercises. The practice of Tai Chi Chi Kung awakens and circulates chi energy and is therefore the foundation for the mastery of Tai Chi Chuan. The potential to develop our self-healing capabilities begins with the discovery of the flow of this vital energy through the Microcosmmic Orbit. This circulation is enhanced and sustained through the practice of Tai Chi Chi Kung which assists in improving health through correct posture, movements and calming of the mind. This particular form is comprised of 13 movements. Prerequisite: Course No. 1 — Opening the Microcosmic Orbit. (Course No. 6)

DAH UH GONG NEI KUNG
FIVE FINGER KUNG FU

The Dah Uh Gong Nei Kung system integrates both static and dynamic exercise forms in order to cultivate and nourish chi which accumulates in the organs, penetrates the fascia, tendons and muscles and, finally reaches the hands and fingers. Practitioners of body-centered therapies and various Healing Arts such as chiropractic medicine, polarity therapy, shiatsu and Swedish massage will benefit from this technique. Practiced sequentially, it functions to expand and relax the breath, calm the mind and adjust posture. The approach is simpler to learn than Tai Chi Chuan and easier to execute than yoga. Through the practice of Dah Uh Gong the student will learn:

- To expand your breathing capacity
- To strengthen your internal organs
- To tone and stretch your muscles
- To strengthen your lower back and abdominal muscles
- To normalize your weight
- To develop your ability to concentrate for self-healing

Prerequisite: Course No. 1 — Opening the Microcosmic Orbit (Course No. 5)

SEMINAL AND OVARIAN KUNG FU

This ancient Taoist yoga practice sublimates and transforms sexual energy through its circulation in the Microcosmic Orbit. The conservation of this precious, biochemical force has been recognized by sages of various esoteric traditions as a major revitalizing factor in the physical health and spiritual development of both men and women. The turning back and circulation of this generative force from the sexual energy centers to the higher centers invigorates and rejuvenates all the body's vital functions. Real sexual fulfillment lies in preventing the indisscriminate loss of this vital current and in experiencing a deeper level of orgasm. These techniques can be used for personal transformation — both physical and spiritual. Prerequisite: Course No. 1 — Opening the Microcosmic Orbit (Course No. 7)

TAI CHI CHUAN — LONG AND SHORT FORMS

In order to benefit from the still, slow and soft movements of the Tai Chi Chuan form, it is necessary for one to have cultivated an awareness of chi and internal power through the Opening of the Microcosmic Orbit and Tai Chi Chi Kung. The Tai Chi Chuan form further educates the body to serve the mind through relaxing and strengthening. In addition, Tai Chi Chuan can be used as a self-defense technique, but only if one is able to properly circulate and utilize the intrinsic energy called chi so that every movement of the body is guided by internal power.

Before beginning to study the Tai Chi Chuan form, the student must have completed:

1) Opening of the Microcosmic Orbit;
2) Tai Chi Chi Kung (13 movements);
3) Iron Shirt Chi Kung Level 1;
4) Seminal and Ovarian Kung Fu Level 1.

(Course Nos. 11 and 12)

The staff includes western M.D.s, nutritionists etc. Master Chia regularly visits each center to lecture and individually counsel Taoist practitioners. He also aides all students in increasing their circulation of chi by "passing energy", especially to those who for whatever reason feel blocked. This is not "instant enlightenment", only an experience of higher chi flow so that the student may better learn to create it on his own.

Future volumes of the Esoteric Taoist Yoga Encyclopedia will explore in depth these other ancient disciplines whose methods have largely been kept secret from westerners.

SEMINAL KUNG FU:
THE TAOIST SECRET OF ENERGY

For more than 5,000 years of Chinese history, "the no outlet method" of retaining the seminal fluid during the act of love has remained a deep secret. At first it was practiced exclusively by the Emperor and his innermost circle. Then it passed from father to chosen son alone, excluding wives, daughters and other family members. The method permits a man to retain bodily secretions which are an invaluable source of energy when stored and recirculated to the vital centers.

Sages of all time and places have found that conservation of the precious energies of the seminal fluid and ovarian energy deeply affects a man's life. Whoever holds his vital seed finds that he spontaneously seeks to preserve living things from waste, decay and harm. On the other hand, those who excessively spend the fluid and its vital force crave outer stimulation at any price, for they desperately need to replace their own lost energies.

One prevents loss of this biochemical energy by not ejaculating. Stopping ejaculation is not to be confused with stopping orgasm. The No Outlet Method provides an altogether unique and superior type of orgasm.

Every vital function is invigorated because one no longer discharges life energy through the genitals. Real sexual fulfillment lies not in feeling the life go out of you but in increasing awareness of the vital current that flows through the loins. The body is further replenished by a method of "Steaming" the vital energy up from the sexual centers to the brain and higher organs. The life enhancing process is completed by exchanging with one's partner energy released during moments of excitation.

The sages have considered one drop of semen equal in vital power to one hundred drops of blood. The Indians refer repeatedly to "Amrito", the elixir of life, a rejuvenating substance from sexual energy. The production of this elixir, which Westerners would call a higher hormonal secretion, allows the body to enter higher and higher states of energy.

Most people in our consumer society spend more than they earn. They borrow themselves deep into debt. Through poor habits they also spend more vital power than they earn.

Let us say that people earn 100 units of life force through breathing, eating and resting but spend 125 units of life force through gluttony, overwork, anxiety, constitutional weakness, and frequent loss of the vital fluid. They must continuously borrow vitality from the brain and other vital organs. This theft of vital energy from one's own reserves induces mental and physical sickness and premature aging. We teach you how to overcome worldly sex desire and a way to earn 125 units and to spend 100 or less. The imbalance of one's personal energy economy is first corrected by reducing the disastrously wasteful expenditure called ejaculation, while experiencing a nourishing balanced energy exchange with one's partner.

IRON SHIRT CHI KUNG

Before guns were used, the Chinese depended very much upon Kung Fu. It is at that time, about one-tenth of the Chinese nation was involved in such practice, which they engaged in from what is found at the present. At first one had to develop internal power — to get the warm current (energy), to open the Microcosmic Circulation, complete another six special channels (routes) and an additional 24 normal channels (routes) so that the internal power could be circulated freely. One then learned how to strengthen one's vital organs and to protect them with internal power or "Iron Shirt". Only then did one go on to practice fighting styles because without internal power the styles were not effective in combat.

It is written that internal power took many years to develop. One had to throw a straight punch up to 2,000 times a day for from three to five years or strike the top of a water well 1,000 times a day for as much as ten years or until the water was thrown out by the force of the blow.

The main purpose of the Iron Shirt is not for fighting, but to perfect the body, to win great health, to fight disease and to protect the vital organs from injuries. Most important in Iron Shirt training is Changing the Tendons & Cleansing the Marrow, and the Self-Regenerative Hormone!

Level I:
- Iron Shirt Chi Kung breathing.
- Awakening and circulating of internal (chi) and rooting power through exercise.
- Directing the internal power to strengthen the organs.
- Filling the 12 tendon channels with chi.
- Training and opening the fascia and filling them with chi.

Level II:
- Cleansing the marrow.
- Changing the tendons and cleansing the marrow.
- Training and opening the fascia and filling them with chi.
- Self-stimulation of the vital organs.
- Strengthening the tendon and uniting the fascia, tendons, bones and muscles in one piece.

Level III:
- Regenerating sexual hormones.
- Storing sexual hormones in the fascia and tendons.
- Directing the internal power to the higher energy centers.

After these three levels of Iron Shirt Chi Kung are mastered, the powerful application of the resulting energy is taught in ''Healing Hand.''

HEALING HAND

a. Buddha palm
b. Pa-Kua palm
c. Checking the Aura and weak energy field
d. Correct and harmonize the circulation system, lymph system, nervous system, chi flow system
e. Point to stop pain and stress

TRANSMITTING THE POWER TO HELP OPEN THE CHANNELS

a. Gathering the power to the palm and finger
b. Restoring the power
c. Transmitting the wet sickness and the cold energy away

DIAGRAM 31
Complementary Taoist Practices

For further information on Taoist Esoteric Yoga Centers in San Diego, Denver, Colorado, Los Angeles and New York City contact:

Healing Tao of the Taoist Esoteric Yoga Center
P.O. Box 1194
Huntington, N.Y. 11743
(516) 367-2701

APPENDIX

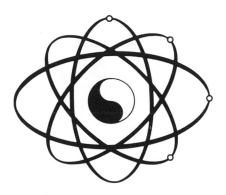

APPENDIX A:

TABLE OF ENERGY CENTERS

NO.	Energy Center Chinese	Acupuncture Name, No.	Chakra, Personality Type	Endocrine Secretions	Color
1.	Tan T'ien	Chi-Chung, CO-8 Umbilicus	Swadisthana Over The Spleen. Social Splenic Plexus Hypogastricus	Spleen	Orange
2.	Sperm Palace Jing Gong	Chung-Chi, CO-3 Four tsun below the umbilicus	Muladhara genital sacral Physical sensation	Prostate gland, seminal vesicle	Red
	Kuan-Yuan	Kuan-Yuan CO-4 Three tsun below the navel, female ovaries energy center.	level, Gonads	Ovaries	

3.	Gate of Mortality Door of Death & Life (Sheng Szu Ch'iao) Testes	Hui-Yin, CO-1 In the center of the perineum, midway between anus & scrotum in the male, and the posterior labial commissure in the female.	Genital-Sacral	Bulbourethral gland, ending of the nerves, vessels, testes	Red
4.	Woei Liu	Chang-Chiang, CO-1 At the lower end of the coccyx between the tip of the cocyx and the anus.	Coccygeal, Sacral Base of the Spine the Root Chakra	Coccygeal Body	
5.	Door of Life	Ming Men, CO-4 Between the spinous process of the 2nd & 3rd lumbar vertebrae, at the midline.	Swadisthana	Kidney	Orange
6.	Jai-Ji	Chi-Chung, CO-6 below the spinous process of the T11th vertebra.	Manipura Pancreas, Solar Plexus, Intellectual Coeliac.	Adrenal	Yellow

NO. Energy Center Chinese	Acupuncture Name, No.	Chakra, Personality Type	Endocrine Secretions	Color
7. Yu-Chen The Jade Pillow	Yu-Chen, BL-9 On the lateral part of the upper margin of the external occipital protuberance and opposite Tien-Chu, BL-10		Medulla, Cerebellum	Blue
8. Niwan Kung Huang-Gong (Yellow Palace)	Pai-Hui, GO-20 At the point of intersectional line joining upper tip of ears and a line from the middle of the forehead directly toward the vertex.	Sahasrara, Crown Imaginative, Brain Absorbing the Yang (heavenly energy) The door spirit.	Pineal	Violet
9. T'ien-T'ing	In the mid point of the forehead.		Hypothalamus	

			Gland	Color
10. Tsu Ch'iao Original Cavity of spirit. The gateway to heaven. Heaven and Earth Yu Ting, Cauldron.	Yin-T'ang, CL-1 Midway between the two eyebrows, in the center of the the brain.	Ajna, Brow Intuitive, Pituitary Carotid.	Pituitary	Indigo
11. Shan-ken (root of the mountain)	At the middle of the two eyes at the root of the nose			
12. Chuen Tou Su-Liao	On the tip of the nose.			
13. Heavenly Pool T'ien chih hsueh Hsuan ying cavity	About 1.5 inches Behind the teeth on the palate; behind the heavenly pool	Mysterious bridle		

NO.	Energy Center Chinese	Acupuncture Name, No.	Chakra, Personality Type	Endocrine Secretions	Color
14.	Twelve Story Shyr Ell Jong Lou	Hsuan-Chi, CO-21 On the Midline of the sternum	Vissuddha, Throat Conceptual, pharyngeal, Plexus Cervicus	Thyroid, Parathyroid	Blue
15.	Gentleman Palace (Jiun Juu Gong) Shin Gong	Shan-Chung, CO-17 Midway between the two nipples, on the level with the 4th intercostal space.	Anahata, Heart Acquisitive Cardiac	Thymus Heart Bodies	Green
16.	Huangting Gong Middle Tan T'ien (Yellow Hall Center) Chung Gong (Middle palace) Dan Gong	Chung-Wan, CO-12 Midpoint on a line connecting the xyphoid process with the umbilicus.	Manipura, Solar Plexus Intellectual, Coeliac, Solar Plexus, Epigastrecus	Pancreas	Yellow

17	Wei-Chung	Wei-Chung, BL-40 In the exact center of the popliteal fossa.	Soul, energy store center
18.	Yung Ch'uan	Yung Ch'uan, K-1 One third the distance from the center of the plata to the front of it and in the depression, which is present when the foot is elevated.	Held to strengthen the kidneys, direct the energy to run down, place for absorbing the Yin (earth energy) collect the energy radiated out from the body.
19.	Ta-Tun	Ta-Tun, Li-1 On the lateral side of the distal phalanx of the great toe posterior to the corner of the vallum unguis. This is the Liver Meridian, regulates the liver.	

NO.	Energy Center Chinese	Acupuncture Name, No.	Chakra, Personality Type	Endocrine Secretions	Color
20.		Yin-Pai, SP-1 On the medial side of the great toe. 0.1 Cun posterior to the corner of nail. This is the spleen meridian, meditation on this will help to regulate the spleen.			
21.	Heding	Heding (Extra 31) On the midpoint of the upper border of the patella (knee cap).	Energy stop center		
22.	Gau Wan Gong Outer kidney	Testes: in external scrotum.	Storage of Yin energy		
23.	Tai-Yang	Tai-yang, CL-2 Midpoint on a line joining the temporal canthus with the lateral eyebrow margin.			

24. Lao-Kung

Lao-Kung, EH-8
At a point between the
2nd and 3rd metocarpal
bones where the 1 tip of
the middle finger
touches when fist is
clenched. Belongs to the
Pericardium Meridian.

DIAGRAM 32
Points & Energy Centers

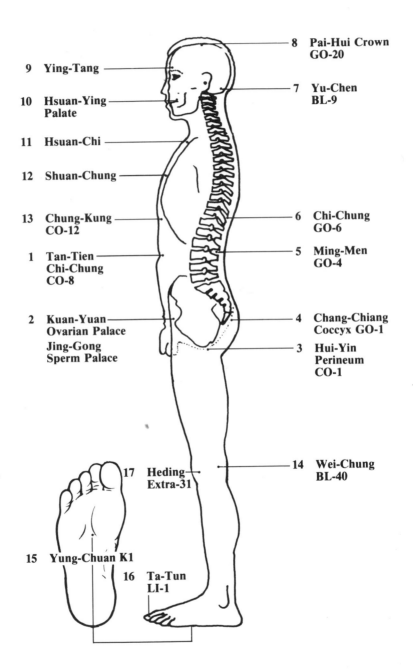

9   Ying-Tang

10   Hsuan-Ying
Palate

11   Hsuan-Chi

12   Shuan-Chung

13   Chung-Kung
CO-12

1   Tan-Tien
Chi-Chung
CO-8

2   Kuan-Yuan
Ovarian Palace
Jing-Gong
Sperm Palace

8   Pai-Hui Crown
GO-20

7   Yu-Chen
BL-9

6   Chi-Chung
GO-6

5   Ming-Men
GO-4

4   Chang-Chiang
Coccyx GO-1

3   Hui-Yin
Perineum
CO-1

14   Wei-Chung
BL-40

17   Heding
Extra-31

15   Yung-Chuan K1

16   Ta-Tun
LI-1

APPENDIX B:

HOW TAOIST YOGA AFFECTS YOUR
HORMONAL SYSTEM

THE ENDOCRINE GLANDS AND
TAOIST ENERGY CENTERS

The hormones are chemical messengers produced by the endocrine glands in minute quantities but eventually affecting every single cell of your body. The secretions of the endocrine glands empty directly into the blood where they find their way to various organs, stimulating or suppressing them, or in some way influencing their activity.

In the Taoist Esoteric System the energy centers do not belong to the physical body at all but are regarded as adjuncts of the "vital body", which are set apart and crystallized to the necessary density in order that it may perform certain special manifestations of this vital body. Each gland has a specific work to perform. When in good health they all work together in perfect harmony. The endocrine glands are of special interest to the students of Taoism in relation to the circulation of the Microcosmic Orbit.

In order to explain some of the energy centers in terms of modern anatomy, one has to look to the endocrine glands for correlation. The correlations may or may not be right, but that is the best that one can hypothesize at this stage of the art.

THE ADRENALS

The adrenals are a pair of glands capping the upper ends of the kidneys. When they are removed, death ensues rapidly. The gland is composed of a cortex (outer portion) and a medulla (inner portion). The outer portion produces the sex steroids, the glucocorticoids (corticosterone, hydrocortisone) which are involved in the control of carbohydrate, lipid and protein metabolism and the mineralocorticoids (aldosterone, deoxycorti-kidney tubules, affecting blood volume and blood pressure control. The adrenals are flat triangular structures. The size and weight is somewhat variable. Each is about 5 cm long and weighs between 3 and 6 grams and is slightly heavier in the male than in the female.

The inner portion of the adrenals is developed from the ectoderm, the outer layer of cells of the embryo. This is the same tissue that produces the sympathetic nervous system. The inner portion secretes adrenalin and noradrenalin. Adrenalin is involved in the "fight or flight" response, whereas noradrenalin causes more vasoconstriction resulting in marked elevation in blood pressure.

The amount of adrenaline and noradrenalin that circulates in the blood is minute in quantity but its action is powerful and far-reaching. It's release is triggered by impulses from the sympathetic nervous system in times of mental or physical stress. the entry of adrenalin into the blood causes a tremendous heightening of vigor. The brain and the sympathetic nervous system become activated. Concentration of blood glucose is raised by conversion from glycogen, which is stored in the liver. More blood cells are poured into circulation from the blood pools of the liver and spleen. The heart beats more strongly and faster, the pupils of the eyes are dilated, enabling the person to see more clearly, breathing is more rapid, the body temperature rises and the basal metabolism is increased. There is an opposing effect on the digestive system, however, wherein there is a loss of appetite and reduced motility.

Adrenalin adds strength and alertness to both physical and mental activity. It gives force in combat and swiftness in flight. As the activity of adrenalin is regulated by the sympathetic nervous system, the secretion of it can be increased by the stimulation of these nerves alongside the spinal column.

Some doctors believe that there is a condition called "low adrenals". A person with a deficiency of adrenalin will appear weary and sensitive to cold, have cold hands and feet, loss of appetite, a tendency to worry, will weep easily and will sometimes even have a nervous breakdown. In children, learning problems develop, growth is slowed, and they cannot be driven or huried.

If we inject someone with adrenalin, his heart will contract more violently and beat faster, he will feel anxious, and will get frightened easily and, if subjected to it for some time, will become a very nervous person.

It is obvious, then, that an intricate, delicate balance of various factors is involved in maintaining a proper harmony of the activities of the various organ systems.

In the Tao Esoteric System, the center for adrenal activity is to be found in the Chi-Chung. This is a very powerful energy center and is located in the area that is called the "solar plexus", which corresponds anatomically to the location of the adrenals, the spleen, the pancreas and the kidneys.

THE KIDNEY

The human kidney is a bean-shaped organ weighing about half a pound. We have two kidneys located within the abdominal cavity and protected at the rear by the spinal column and the big muscles of the back. The tops of the kidneys are just beneath the ribcage. The right kidney, above which lies the liver, is usually a little lower than the left. About 1,700 quarts of blood flow through the kidneys each day.

Among the kidney cells are certain glands of endocrine secretion. The kidneys produce blood-pressure-elevating substances causing hypertension at times. Erythropoietin is a substance produced by some kidney cells, that stimulates the production of red blood cells.

In the Taoist Esoteric System, the Ming-men (the Door of Life) is the energy center corresponding to the activity of the kidneys.

DIAGRAM 33
The Endocrine Glands

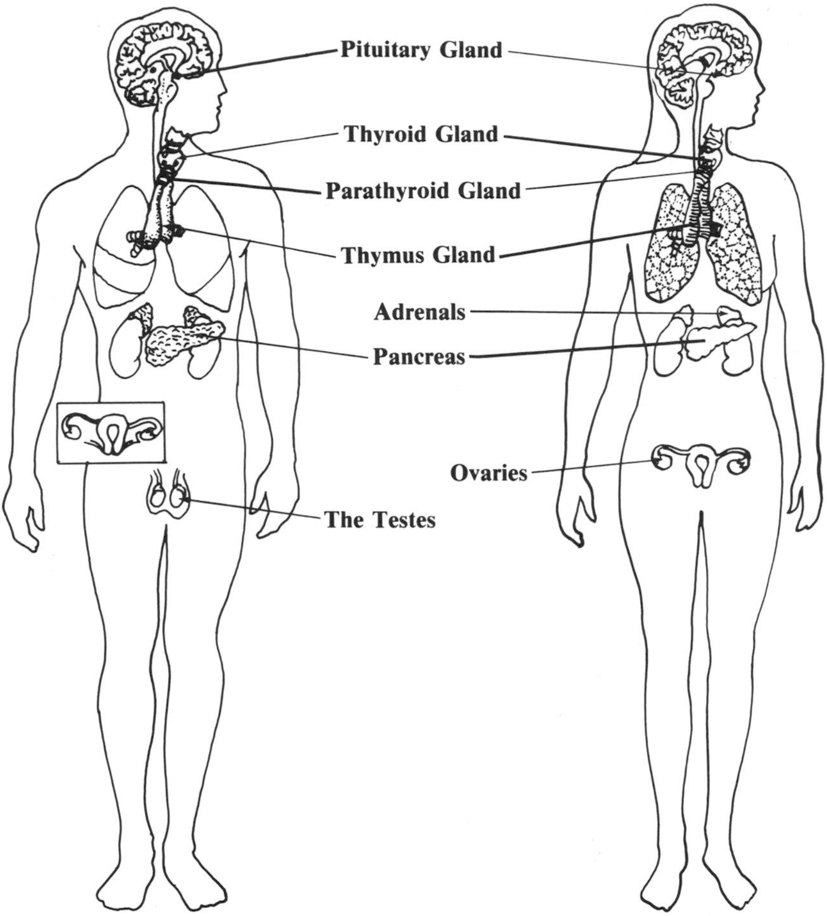

Pituitary Gland

Thyroid Gland

Parathyroid Gland

Thymus Gland

Adrenals

Pancreas

Ovaries

The Testes

THE TESTES

The male gonads or testes lie in the scrotal sac and the normal size varies from that of a walnut to that of a pigeon egg. There are two parts to the testes, the tubules, which produce the sperm, and the Leydig cells, which produce the principal masculinizing hormone, testosterone. Leydig cells also produce small amounts of estrogens, the female sex hormones.

The testicle is under the control of gonad-stimulating hormones or Gonadotrophins. Just before the onset of puberty, gonadotrophins are released, causing the testes to mature and to secrete increasing amounts of testosterone. This induces development of the secondary sex characteristics such as development of the penis, pubic and auxiliary hair growth, increased muscle mass, voice changes, beard growth and all the signs of manliness in vigor and perhaps even influencing deportment and behavior.

With adequate gonadotrophins and androgen production, the tubular germ cells ripen into sperm cells.

In the case of disorders of the testes, secondary sexual characteristics will not develop if there is an androgen deficiency during puberty. If this occurs after maturity, a partial regression occurs. A pituitary disease may be the cause of this deficiency also.

In the Taoist Esoteric System, we believe that there is tremendous potential in the energy of the sperm and sex hormones. We awaken and transform this energy to the higher centers.

THE OVARIES

The ovaries, like the testes, have two functions: first, to provide ova or egg cells and secondly, to secrete sex hormones. The hormones of the ovaries are estrogens and progesterone and unusual conditions androgens may be produced.

The ovaries are awakened to activity when a young girl reaches 11 to 13 years of age. The "female" hormones serve to develop the secondary feminine sex characteristics of breast growth, pubic and auxiliary hair, maturation of the genital tract and also the contours of the female figure, and many contribute to the psychological characteristics of the woman.

Inadequate or absent ovarian stimulation by the pituitary gonadotrophic hormones, failure of the ovary to respond, or an abnormal response to the stimulation, results in many disorders ranging from inborn failure to menstruate, subsequent cessation of menses and development of male characteristics.

In the Taoist system, we regard the ovaries as one of the great energy centers of the female. The female can awaken and transform the great energy from the ovaries to the higher center.

THE SPLEEN

The spleen is located beyond the left end of the stomach, between it and the diaphragm. It is bean-shaped and has a deep blue-red color. It weighs from five to six ounces and is soft, spongy, and fragile. The spleen controls blood destruction.

IN THE TAOIST ESOTERIC SYSTEM WE REGARD THE SPLEEN AS THE ENTRANCE FOR SOLAR FORCE, WHICH VITALIZES THE DENSE BODY. Without this vital elixir no being can live. From the spleen this sun force is sent to the solar plexus and from the solar plexus this fluid-like energy flows along the filaments composing the nervous system. In this way it permeates every part of the physical body. energizing each and every cell with its life force.

According to Chinese medicinal theories, when a person is healthy, life energy is stored by the spleen and extracted from the blood in such large quantities that it cannot be used inside the body. Therefore, the life energy radiates outward through the pores of the skin in straight lines, drives out poisonous gases, inimical bacteria and viruses and assists in preserving a healthy condition of the physical organism. It also prevents armies of disease germs which swarm about in the atmosphere from entering the dense vehicle.

According to the Taoist system, after eating, the vital solar force attracted by the spleen is consumed by the body in great quantities. When the meal is heavy, the outflow of the vital fluid from the body is perceptibly diminished and does not then cleanse the dense vehicle as thoroughly as it does when the food has been digested, nor is it as potent in keeping out inimical germs. Therefore, overeating renders a person more likely to catch cold or succumb to disease. During ill health the spleen furnishes the vital body with very little solar energy, and at this time the dense body seems to feed on the vital body. In the Taoist system it is said that we have to repair the vital body, which can then help the dense body to get stronger.

In Taoist Esoterica, the "solar plexus" is regarded as the largest cauldron of the vital body which can alchemically mix or harmonize the generative force with the life energy from the energy center corresponding to the pituitary gland, during the practice of Greater Enlightenment of the Kan and Li. The spleen, as mentioned before, corresponds to a part of the "solar plexus."

THE THYMUS GLAND

This is the gland of child development. It is situated in the chest between the lungs and behind the upper part of the sternum (breast bone). It descends and covers the upper portion of the heart, overlapping the great vessels at the top of the latter. It reaches its greatest size at the beginning of puberty, gradually disappearing thereafter at which time it is marked by a loss of glandular structure. It does persist, however, and some of the secreting cells remain throughout life.

In Taoist Yoga, when properly and proportionally activated the energy center at the thymus alchemically harmonizing with the energy from the pituitary gland energy center and the generative force residing in the sperm and testicles, can reverse the aging process. This occurs in the practice of the Greatest Enlightenment of the Kan and Li, in which white hair becomes black, teeth grow back again, and a youthful appearance develops.

THE HYPOTHALAMUS

The hypothalamus is part of the forebrain, the same part of the brain from which the cerebral hemispheres develop. The hypothalamus provides a connecting link between the cerebral cortex and the pituitary gland. Though the pituitary gland is considered the master gland, nevertheless, there are stimulatory and inhibitory agents originating in the hypothalamus, which regulate pituitary functions. This ancient area in our brain is also intimately concerned with the regulation of energy balance through the control of appetite, sleep, body temperature, the regulation of sexual function and control of water balance.

Disturbances in the hypothalamus may cause such endocrine disorders as sexual precocity, absence of appetite with extreme loss of weight, diabetes insipidus and disorganization of the sleep pattern.

Indeed, the hypothalamus and the pituitary gland are both functionally and anatomically related. Our thoughts, our hopes and joys, our worries and our sorrows, our very nervous constitution all profoundly influence the hypothalamus-pituitary complex. In the Taoist Esoteric System, the energy center of Tien-Ting (in the mid-point of the forehead) corresponds to the hypothalamus.

THE THYROID GLAND: THE GLAND OF ENERGY

The thyroid gland is located in the throat and lies in front of and on either side of the windpipe and just beneath the larynx (voice box) and is connected just below the Adam's apple. This gland arises from the same tissue and almost from the same spot as the anterior lobe of the pituitary body. It weighs about an ounce. Each lobe of the thyroid is about two inches in length, and from an inch to an inch and a quarter in width.

The thyroid gland is highly vascularized and receives many times more blood in proportion to its size. It is noted for their high degree of functional activity. It is heavier in the female than in the male and becomes enlargd during sexual excitement, menstruation, and pregnancy.

The thyroid gland's secretion is called thyroxin, which contains idodine.

The thyroid is an energy gland and its secretion is the controller of the speed of living. It affects the metabolism of practically all the tissues of the body. The principal function of the hormone is to regulate the rate of oxygen consumption, which is tantamount to the body's metabolic rate, which can be thought of as one's "rate of living". This hormone is required for normal growth and development of the brian, muscle and bones and it indirectly affects the activity of other glands of internal secretion as well. Too little thyroid hormone produces a condition of sluggishness. With too much, there will be marked apprehension, alertness, nervousness, loss of weight, increased thirst, frequent urination, profuse perspiration, intolerance of heat, insomnia, frequent stools, rapid heartbeat and palpitations.

In the Taoist Approach, the energy center at the thyroid is considered to be one of the most important centers in the body because it controls the growth of the dense vehicle and mental development and it is very closely related to all of the other six energy centers under consideration. It is THE GREAT LINK BETWEEN THE BRAIN AND THE ORGANS OF GENERATION (reproductive organs).

In the Taoist Esoteric System, the thyroid energy center is called Hsuan-Chi (the twelve story) and is used as an energy Center only to draw in power. It is not ordinarily included in alchemy because when it is open it is hard to protect. However, in the GREATER AND THE GREATEST ENLIGHTENMENT OF THE KAN & LI, we draw enormous stores of power from this energy center to alchemically mix with the power of other energy centers in order to produce an ever greater source of power.

THE PITUITARY GLAND

The pituitary gland is about the size of a pea, situated almost exactly in the center of the head at the base of the brain and just behind the root of the nose. It hangs suspended from the underside of the brain like a cherry from the limb of a tree. It is grayish-yellow in color. In the adult it weighs about five grains, or 1/1400 of a pound.

Its name is derived from the Latin word, "pituita", because it was supposed to secret a fluid which lubricated the throat. It was believed that the secretion filtered through the porous ethnoid bone that intervenes between the pituitary body and the nasal cavity.

TONGUE TOUCHES THE PALATE

Embryologically, the pituitary begins by manifesting as an outgrowth of the mouth cavity. This outgrowth takes the form of a pouch, which gradually extends toward the brain. By the end of the fourth week this protrusion contacts a downgrowth from the brain called the infundibulum. The pouch then develops into the anterior lobe of the pituitary, whereas the infundibulum, representing an outgrowth of the oldest part of the nervous system, develops into the posterior lobe of the gland. There is a space between the walls of the anterior and posterior parts of the gland, which persists throughout life as the cleft of the gland.

The pituitary gland is divided into an anterior or front portion, which is composed of glandular tissue and a posterior or back portion, which is composed of nerve-like tissue. The anterior portion produces several hormones which stimulate distant structures such as: a growth hormone, a hormone which stimulates the adrenal cortex, a thyroid stimulating hormone and also a hormone which stimulates breast milk production and another which influences pigment production by certain cells of the skin.

The posterior part of the gland is an extension of the hypothalamus, that portion of the brain to which the pituitary is attached.

The posterior lobe of the pituitary body secretes several important hormones, two of which deserve special attention. One of them, called pitocin, has a powerful stimulating effect on the pregnant uterus and is frequently used in cases where labor is slow and ineffective. The other, called antidiuretic hormone, controls the salt and water content of the blood.

In animal studies, an active pituitary produces alertness. A tired or dull pituitary produces sleepiness and general dullness. During hibernation or winter sleep, an animal in cold weather passes into a cataleptic state in which it continues to breathe, more deeply but more slowly than when awake. The internal secretions of all of the glands of hibernating animals show changes during this period but the most marked effect is found in the pituitary in which the cells shrink as if they too were asleep or resting. When the spring comes, the pituitary gland cells again become normally active.

In the Taoist System, special attention is given to properly stimulate and harmonize the energy center related to this gland. Attempts have been made to mix pituitary gland energy with sources of cooler energy such as sperm and earth power. This constitutes a cauldron for cultivating the spirit in the practice called: THE SEALING OF THE FIVE SENSE ORGANS.

THE PINEAL GLAND
(The Human Compass)

The pineal gland is a cone-shaped body, reddish in color, about half an inch in length, and not much larger than a grain of wheat. It is attached to, and situated over, the third ventricle of the brain, weighing about two grains. It is composed, in part, of nerve cells containing a pigment similar to that present in the cells of the retina. This strengthens the argument for its function as an eye in earlier animal species.

In the Taoist terminology, the Niwan-Kung corresponds to this gland. In the cauldron, it is considered to cultivate the highest level of the spirit in the practice: Congress of Heaven. When the gland is fully developed it will tell us where our destination is.

DIAGRAM 34
The Pituitary Gland

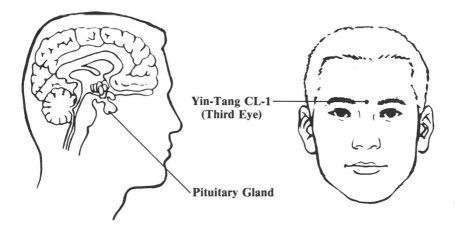

Yin-Tang CL-1
(Third Eye)

Pituitary Gland

AURORA PRESS

THE ELISABETH HAICH SERIES

Through books such as *Initiation*, Elisabeth Haich has become world famous for her profound understanding of the human soul. The Yoga schools she set up in Europe with Selvarajan Yesudian have become internationally renowned.

WISDOM OF THE TAROT
Wisdom of the Tarot relates the path of higher consciousness through the color, shape and symbolic forms on the 22 cards. Detailed study of a Tarot card may release instinctive awareness of each level towards the Light. When studied individually, a card may reveal the necessary steps to find one's essential path. Included are 5 color gold Tarot cards.
Paper 174pp.   **$12.50**

SEXUAL ENERGY & YOGA
This book is to introduce the concept of transmuting the physical emotional psychic mental energy people normally disperse in sexual activity for the purpose of uniting their bodies in their higher Self or God.
Paper 160pp   **$6.95**

THE EAR
Gateway to Balancing the Body
A Modern Guide to Ear Acupuncture
Mario Wexu, D. Ac.
This is the first complete modern textbook of ear acupuncture. Anatomical descriptions with detailed charts clearly illustrate how to locate and use over 300 ear points, both alone and in combination with body points, to treat and prevent illness. An excellent repertory listing 150 diseases facilitates an indepth understanding of this incredible and valuable healing art.
Cloth 203pp.   **$30.00**

COLOR THERAPY
Dr. Reuben Amber
This comprehensive book enumerates the myriad ways we can consciously choose to use color to influence our body, mind, and soul to promote balanced health and well being. No other book includes as thorough a historical survey of Color Therapies along with specific applications of color in all facets of life.
Paper 207pp.   **$9.95**

HOW ATMOSPHERIC CONDITIONS AFFECT YOUR HEALTH
Dr. Michel Gauquelin
A unique exploration by psychologist and statistician Dr. Michel Gauquelin, of the tremendous influence of the cycle of the seasons, range of climates, cosmic clocks, Lunar Cycles, & Sunspots on the complex balance of mental and physical health.
Paper 224pp.   **$8.95**

SELF HEALING, YOGA AND DESTINY
Designed to reconnect you with the Divine, the concepts within this book explain the attitudes necessary for the path back to one's Self. Based on many years personal experience, the author creates a vehicle to realize the essential source of Life, especially in relation to illness and self healing.
Paper 80pp.   **$4.95**

THE DAY WITH YOGA
A different creative energy is at work on each day of the week. In this book Elisabeth Haich has carefully chosen and collected quotations which show us how we can attune to the cosmic vibrations of each day.
Paper 96pp.   **$3.95**

CHART INTERPRETATION —
Astrology and Psychology
Doris Hebel
A compilation of articles on Chart Interpretation, covering Elements, aspects, hemisphere emphasis, retrogrades, stations, parental indicators, and case histories.
Paper 64pp.   **$5.**

SYNASTRY
Understanding Human Relations
Through Astrology   *Ronald Davison*
This book contains the first comprehensive survey of the various techniques of horoscope comparison.

The author has discovered "The Relationship Horoscope," an entirely new way of charting in a single horoscope the relationship between two people. He also introduces new methods of determining the quality of that relationship.
Paper 352pp.   **$10.95**

AWAKEN SELF-HEALING ENERGY THROUGH THE TAO
Mantak Chia
This unique book reveals the ancient Taoist secret of circulating internal energy through acupuncture meridians, for physical, psychological and spiritual health. Written in clear, easy to understand language and illustrated with many detailed diagrams that aid the development of a powerful energetic flow.
Paper 224pp.   **$10.95**

AURORA PRESS

CELESTIAL PSYCHOLOGY
Doris Hebel

A comprehensive investigation of planetary energies and their effect on human consciousness, transcending conventional astrological interpretation and delineation. An in-depth blend of Astrology and Psychology encompassing both the esoteric and exoteric levels of planetary manifestation in human behavior and experience. Included are numerous mental, emotional, physical and spiritual remedial techniques designed to assist in dealing with the implications and complexes inherent in specific planetary combinations.

$8.95

TAOIST SECRETS OF LOVE—CULTIVATING MALE SEXUAL ENERGY
Mantak Chia

The ancient sexual secrets of the Taoist sages enable men to conserve and transform sexual energy through its circulation in the Microcosmic Orbit, invigorating and rejuvenating the body's vital functions. Hidden for centuries, these esoteric techniques and principles make the process of linking sexual energy and transcendent states of consciousness accessible to the reader.

Paper 285pp. $12.50

SILVER DENTAL FILLINGS:
The Toxic Timebomb
Sam Ziff

A significant and shocking exposé of one of the greatest health dangers of our time. The amalgam used to fill teeth is 40 to 50 per cent Mercury. It is explained in this book how it migrates from the teeth into the body affecting our overall health in a dramatic manner. This groundbreaking book includes:

Mercury in medicine and dentistry
The history of mercury in medicine
The arguments for and against
Do we really have electricity in our
    mouths?
Measurement of Mercury in the urine
Mercury in the body, where does it go?
How long does it stay?
Does Mercury cause any changes in our
    tissues and organs?
Fantasy or fact, does Mercury cause psychiatric and behavioral changes?
Micromercurialism, signs and symptoms

This book is written in a clear straightforward manner, ideal for the layman and professional, who wants to become aware of the body of information currently available on Mercury toxicity. Then, informed, each individual can draw their own conclusions.

Paper 168pp. $8.95

AURORA PRESS

Aurora Press is devoted to pioneering books that catalyze personal growth, balance and transformation. Aurora makes available in a digestible format, an innovative synthesis of ancient wisdom with twentieth century resources, integrating esoteric knowledge and daily life.

Recent titles include:

COMING HOME
Deborah Duda

CRYSTAL ENLIGHTENMENT
Katrina Raphaell

CRYSTAL HEALING
Katrina Raphaell

SILVER DENTAL FILLINGS • THE TOXIC TIMEBOMB
Sam Ziff

AWAKEN HEALING ENERGY THROUGH THE TAO
Mantak Chia

TAOIST SECRETS OF LOVE
Mantak Chia

THE LUNATION CYCLE
Dane Rudhyar

SELF HEALING, YOGA AND DESTINY
Elisabeth Haich

For a complete catalog write:

AURORA PRESS
P.O. BOX 573
SANTA FE NEW MEXICO 87504
(505) 989-9804